ACCA

Paper P1

Governance, risk and ethics

Pocket notes

KAPLAN PUBLISHING

British library cataloguing-in-publication data

A catalogue record for this book is available from the British Library.

Published by:
Kaplan Publishing UK
Unit 2 The Business Centre
Molly Millars Lane
Wokingham
Berkshire
RG41 2QZ

ISBN 978-1-78415-246-8

Printed and bound in Great Britain.

Contents

Exam guidance – keys to success in this paper

The aim of this paper is to apply relevant knowledge and skills and to exercise professional judgement in carrying out the role of the accountant relating to governance, internal control, compliance and the management of risk within an organisation, in the context of an overall ethical framework. It is important to remember that this is a Professional level paper and you are expected not only to be able to reproduce the details of a particular code or theory but to be able to discuss the arguments for and against an idea or approach, often in the context of a particular scenario.

Paper P1 Governance, Risk and Ethics is underpinned by Paper F1 Accountant in Business. It is also supported by the new on-line Professional Ethics module which all students registering from January 2007 are required to take, preferably before or at the same time as Paper P1, Governance, Risk and Ethics. If you are an existing student transferring to the new syllabus this module is not compulsory – however you are encouraged to take it to improve your understanding of ethical issues facing accountants. The Ethics Module should also assist you in answering questions on the P1 paper. Further information on the Ethics Module can be found on the ACCA website.

Although the syllabus is divided into five different areas, no area should be viewed in isolation from the others. Corporate governance is a key topical area, but recent high-profile corporate failures have been due to deficiencies in internal control. Effective risk management forms an important part of good governance. An understanding of ethics is also important in explaining how corporate governance failures occur.

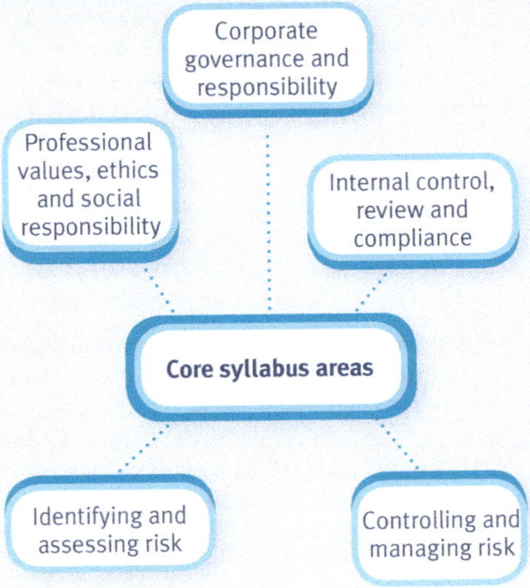

The examination

Exam format

Section A (50%)

- compulsory question
- three to five parts, some with sub-sections
- based on a long scenario and will co[ver] all areas of the syllabus
- will always contain an ethics element and generally a significant amount of corporate governance marks
- four to six professional marks will be available in this question.
- From 2011 be aware of the possibilit[y] of bringing in some simple arithmetic calculations into the Risk area of the syllabus

Section B (50%)

- choice of two questions from three, each worth 25 marks
- more likely to assess a range of subject areas from the main syllabus headings
- short scenarios are likely to be used.

At the beginning of the exam there will be 15 minutes reading and planning time during which you can annotate the question paper.

The syllabus does not ask for knowledge of particular codes with the exception of the Sarbanes-Oxley Act and the OECD and ICGN Reports on corporate governance. However you will be expected to illustrate points with reference to an appropriate code, which may be a local one, to demonstrate your understanding. Although knowledge of the UK's Corporate Governance Code is not required it does provide a very useful basis for answering questions on corporate governance requirements. The ACCA and IFAC codes of ethics are useful for answering questions on ethics and professionalism.

Exam focus

Keys to exam success

- The ability to apply theory to the scenarios given.
- Answering exactly the question that has been set.
- Providing specific and detailed answers.
- Earning professional marks (for presenting answers in section A in the prescribed format, with appropriate style, focus and use of language).
- Addressing the requirement of the verb used in the question.
- Answering both parts of a question requirement (rule of "and").
- Reading examiner's articles published in Student Accountant.

Examination tips

Spend the first few minutes of the examination reading the paper.

Where you have a choice of questions, decide which ones you will do.

Divide the time you spend on questions in proportion to the marks on offer. One suggestion **for this examination** is to allocate 1.8 minutes to each mark available, so a 10-mark section of a question should be completed in approximately 18 minutes.

Spend some time **planning** your answer. Stick to the question and **tailor your answer** to what you are asked. Pay particular attention to the verbs in the question and make sure you identify all the requirements of a question.

Spend the last five minutes reading through your answers and making any additions or corrections.

If you **get completely stuck** with a quest leave space in your answer book and **ret to it later**.

If you do not understand what a question is asking, state your assumptions. Even i you do not answer in precisely the way th examiner hoped, you should be given so credit, if your assumptions are reasonabl

Do everything you can to make things ea for the marker. The marker will find it eas to identify the points you have made if yo answers are legible.

An essay answer should have a clear structure. It should contain a brief introduction, a main section and a conclusion. Be concise. It is better to writ a little about a lot of different points than great deal about one or two points.

In case study questions, first identify th area in which there is a problem, outline main principles/theories you are going to o answer the question, and then apply the rinciples/ theories to the case.

Some questions ask you to present your inswer in the form of a report or other locument. So use the correct format – there could be easy marks to gain here.

Key study tips

Ensure you review prior knowledge from earlier papers.

Revise the course as you work through it and leave sufficient time before the exam for inal revision.

Cover the whole syllabus and pay attention o areas where your knowledge is weak.

Practice exam standard questions under imed conditions.

Read good newspapers and professional ournals. There are many examples of shareholders exerting influence, unethical corporate behaviour and events which are potentially damaging to reputations which you can use to illustrate your answers. Ensure you review the ACCA's Student Accountant for any articles that your examiner may write. These can form the basis of future exam questions.

Quality and accuracy are of the utmost importance to us so if you spot an error in any of our products, please send and email to mykaplanreporting@kaplan.com with full details, or follow the link to the feedback form in MyKaplan.

Our Quality Co-ordinator will work with our technical team to verify the error and take action to ensure it is corrected in future editions.

hapter

1

Theory of governance

In this chapter

- Company ownership and control.
- Corporate governance.
- Business case for governance.
- Key concepts in governance.
- Operational areas affected by issues in corporate governance.
- Internal and external stakeholders.
- Public Sector governance.
- Agency theory.
- Principal-agent relationships and corporate governance.
- Cost of agency relationships.
- Agency problem resolution measures.
- Transaction cost theory.
- Stakeholder theory.

Company ownership and control

- Spilt between ownership and control in companies.

Ownership	**Control**
Shareholders own shares in company	Directors run company for shareholders

- Gives rise to agency problems.
- Joint-stock company is a company which issues shares.

Corporate governance

- Corporate governance is the system by which companies are directed and controlled in the interests of shareholders and other stakeholders.

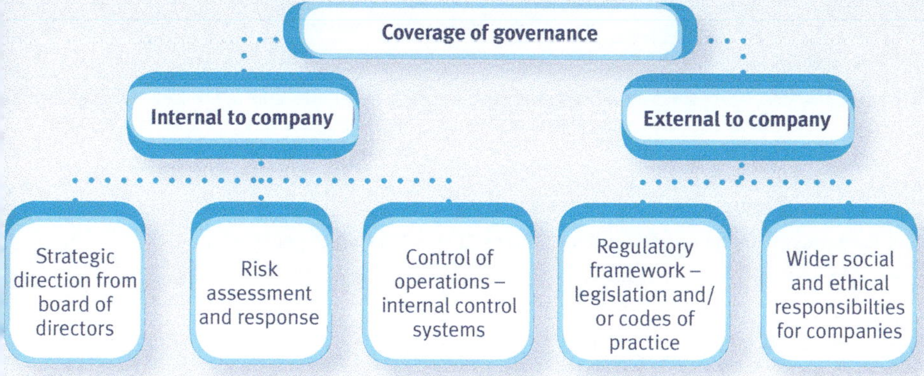
Coverage of governance
Internal to company
External to company
Strategic direction from board of directors
Risk assessment and response
Control of operations – internal control systems
Regulatory framework – legislation and/ or codes of practice
Wider social and ethical responsibilties for companies

Corporate governance	
Purpose	**Objectives**
Monitor those parties within a company who control the resources owned by investors.	Contribute to improved corporate performan and accountability in creating long-term shareholder value.

Business case for governance

- Increases accountability and maximises sustainable wealth creation.
- More attractive to investors.
- Governance dividend in share price.
- Social responsibility dividend.

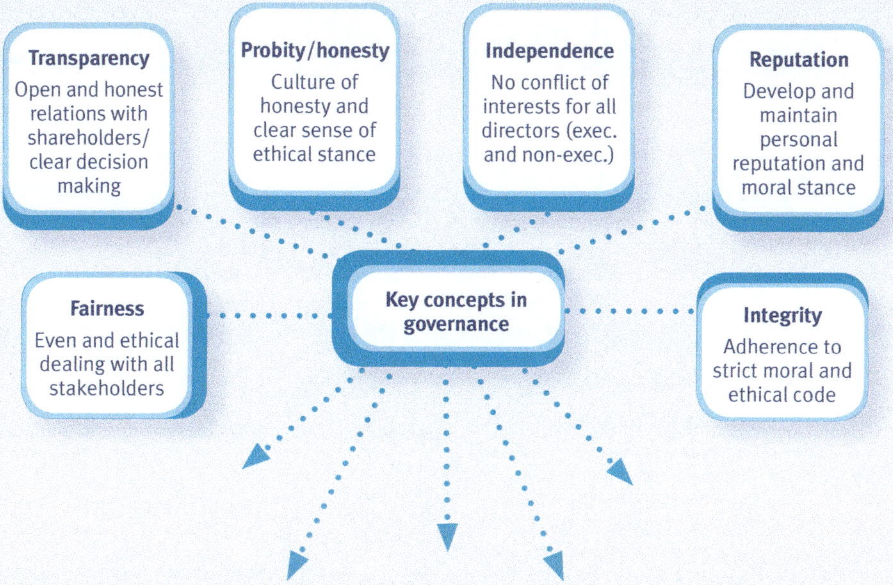
Transparency
Open and honest relations with shareholders/ clear decision making
Probity/honesty
Culture of honesty and clear sense of ethical stance
Independence
No conflict of interests for all directors (exec. and non-exec.)
Reputation
Develop and maintain personal reputation and moral stance
Fairness
Even and ethical dealing with all stakeholders
Key concepts in governance
Integrity
Adherence to strict moral and ethical code

Innovation

- Innovation and experimentation in reporting
- The business moves away from rigid compliance towards the better communication of its individual value creation story for its providers of financial capital

Accountability

Provision of compl
information to al
stakeholders an
effective risk
management

Responsibility

- Acceptance of responsibility for governance decisions
- Clarity or roles and responsibilities

Judgement

Ability to make correct decision from many conflicting inputs

Scepticism

- Scepticism(often referred to as professional scepticism) is an attitude which include a questioning mind
- To provide a critical assessment of evidence
- For example, non-executive directors apply scepticism in order to challenge and scrutinise management effectively

Exam focus

You will need to be able to define any of the key concepts for two marks in the exam. These are examined by a definition and then some application or discussion in the context of a scenario. For example, transparency vs. the need for confidentiality in a commercial situation.

Operational areas affected by issues in corporate governance

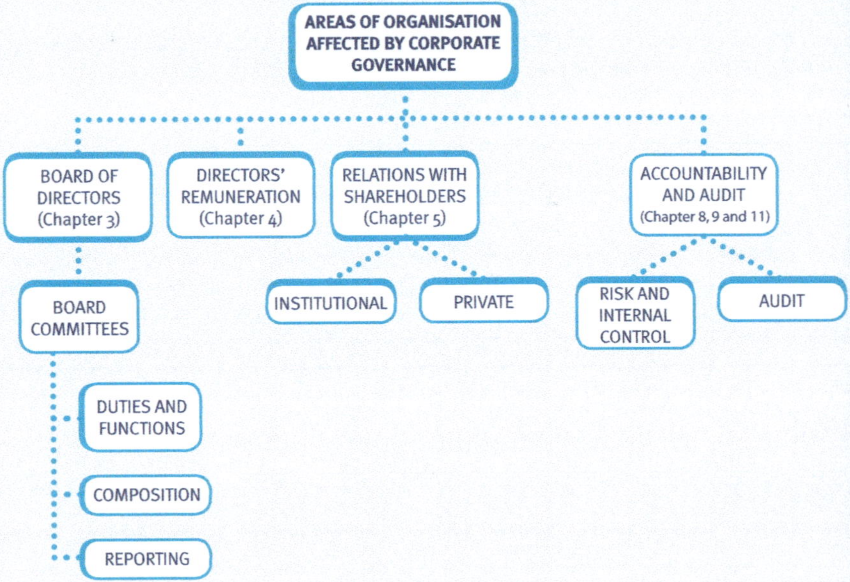

Internal and external stakeholders

Internal		External	
Directors	Control company in best interests of stakeholders.	Auditors	Independent review of company's reported financial position.
Company Secretary	Ensure compliance with company legislation. Advise board in corporate governance matters.	Regulators	Implementing and monitoring regulations.
		Government	Implementing and maintaining laws with which all companies must comply
Sub-board management	Run business operations. Implement board policies.	Stock exchange	Implementing and maintaining rules and regulations for companies listed on the exchange.
Employees	Carry out orders of management.		
Employee representatives e.g. Trade unions	Protect employee interests.	Institutional investors	Make considered use of their votes.

Public Sector governance

A range of organisations exists in most economies with three types predominant.

Private sector – exist to make a profit.

Charities – which are charitable or benevolent.

Public sector – delivering goods or services not be provided by "for profit" entities.

The latter are operated predominantly by the state (self governing autonomous region), made up of four aspects.

- The government – an elected body.
- The legislature – e.g. in the UK Houses of Parliament.
- The judiciary – independently appointed.
- The secretariat – separate administrative body to carry out state functions e.g. Education.

The problem of agency in the Public Sector

Those that manage a business (the agen do not own that business but manage the business on behalf of those who do own (the principals), The key concept of agen in the context of corporate governance. In the public sector, the principals are different and rather than being for examp shareholders are often those that fund ar use the activity.

Funders and service users are therefore sometimes the same people (i.e. taxpaye placing their children in state school) but often they are not, giving rise to disagreements on how much is spent an what service provision.

Public sector organisations are therefore more concerned with delivering their serv efficiently, effectively and to achieve goo value for money.

Their objectives can therefore be more complex to develop.

This is often depicted as the three E's:

- Economy – to deliver the service on time and within budget.
- Effectiveness – to deliver the service the organisation was created to provide.
- Efficiency – gaining an acceptable return on the money invested.

Governance arrangements in the Public Sector

No one single mechanism being appropriate to control and monitor the achievement of objectives, accountability is achieved by having a system of reporting and oversight.

This entails those in charge of the service delivery to report to an external body of oversight which may be e.g. a board of governors or trustees.

The oversight body acts in the interest of the providers of finance, the taxpayer to ensure that the service is delivered on time and is for the benefit of the users.

Membership may include executive and non-executive positions similar to the private sector.

The roles of the oversight bodies include:

- To ensure the service complies with government rules
- To ensure that performance targets are met
- To set and monitor performance against budgets
- To oversee senior appointments
- To monitor management performance
- To remove underperforming senior managers
- To report to higher authorities on the organisations being monitored.

Agency theory

Agency theory

- examines the duties and conflicts that occur between parties who have an agency relationship
- occurs when one party, the principal, employs another party, the agent, to perform a task on their behalf
- is relevant to companies – shareholders = principal directors = agents
- incorporates the fiduciary relationship that exists between the principal and the agent.

Agent is accountable to principals for their actions e.g. directors running the company for shareholders benefit.

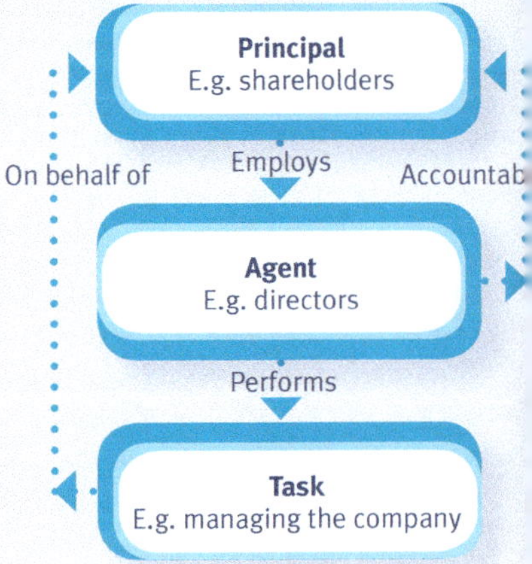

Principal-agent relationships and corporate governance

The principal-agent problem – separation of ownership and control leads to conflict of interest.

Relationship	Problem	Resolution
Shareholders/ directors	Directors vote large salaries/expensive cars	• Meetings between directors/ principle shareholders • Voting at AGM
Shareholders/ auditors	Auditors not independent of directors; may not produce appropriate audit report	• Audit committee recommend appointment • Ethical rules

Cost of agency relationships

Agency costs

- principal's monitoring activities of agents
- money, resources consumed or time taken
- borne by principal.

Residual loss

- additional type of agency cost
- costs above the remuneration package for a director
- direct loss to shareholders.

Exam focus

Anything that can improve the trusting relationship between shareholders and directors will reduce agency costs, such a
improved voluntary disclosure.

Agency problem resolution measures

- meetings between directors and key institutional shareholders
- voting rights at the AGM in support of, or against, resolutions
- proposing resolutions for vote by shareholders at AGMs
- accepting takeovers
- divestment of shares.

Transaction cost theory

Transaction costs occur when dealing with another party.

Costs occur	Costs are • Search and information • Bargaining and decision • Policing and enforcement
Analysis of costs limited by	• Bounded rationality (lack of information) • Opportunism (satisfying own interests)
Factors affecting decision	• Frequency of use of service • Level of uncertainty • Asset specificity – unique component?

Conclusions from transaction cost theory

- Businesses organise themselves to minimise impact of bounded rationality and opportunism.
- Governance costs rise as monitoring increases.
- Managers become more risk averse.

Transaction cost theory vs. agency theory

- Transaction cost theory focuses on individual transaction as opposed to individual agent.
- Both consider directors' tendency to act in their own interests.
- Transaction cost theory aims to achieve effective and efficient transactions by firms.

Stakeholder theory

- Companies have responsibilities to more groups than just shareholders.
- 'Stake' suggests exchange relationship – parties exchange benefits.
- E.g. government builds road for company: company pays taxes + does not pollute environment.

Exam focus

Stakeholder theory is a popular topic in this exam, and will be revisited in subsequent chapters. The examiner wrote two articles on stakeholders in 2008 which are essential reading.

Stakeholder theory and agency theory

- Agency theory narrow form of stakeho theory.
- Stakeholder theory relevant to compa because it is a business case for considering the interests of stakeholde
- Both theories attempt to align interests two parties.

Exam focus

Recent P1 questions on this topic include:

Topic	Pilot	D07	J08	D08	J09	DO9	J10	D10	J11	D11	J12	D12	J13	D13	J14	D14
Concepts	Q3	Q1	Q1				Q1	Q1	Q3		Q2	Q2	Q4	Q2	Q1	
Agency theory	SPQ3	Q4	Q3		Q1		Q1				Q1					
Public sector governance																Q2

*SP refers to supplementary pilot question paper

hapter

2

Development of corporate governance

In this chapter

- Influences on corporate governance.
- Development of corporate governance (UK).
- UK Corporate Governance Code.
- Developing governance codes.

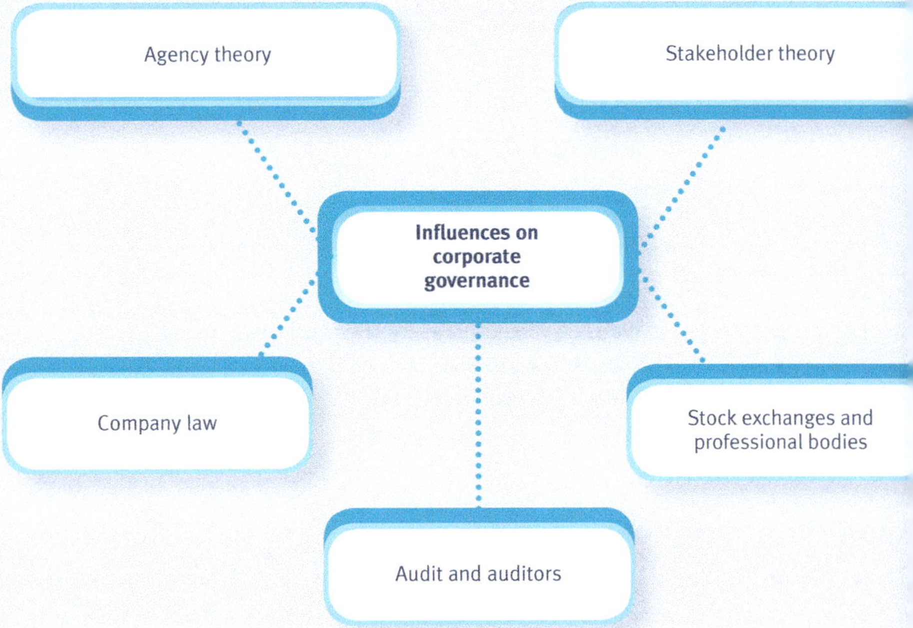
Agency theory
Stakeholder theory
Influences on corporate governance
Company law
Stock exchanges and professional bodies
Audit and auditors

Development of corporate governance (UK)

Date	Report	Key areas
1992	Cadbury	• Board of directors – to be monitored, chairman/CEO role to be split • Institutional investors – need for greater dialogue • Audit and accountability – good communication and disclosure
1995	Greenbury	• Directors' remuneration – balance between salary and performance
1998	Hampel	• Combined Code providing principles of good corporate governance
1999	Turnbull	• Need for appropriate internal control systems
2003	Higgs	• Role of non-executive directors – represent shareholders, cautionary voice
2003	Tyson	• Recruitment and development of NEDs
2003	Smith	• Auditors and audit committees
2003	Financial Reporting Council	• Re-draft of Combined Code
2010	Financial Reporting Council	• Name changed to The UK Corporate Governance Code and sections redrafted

UK Corporate Governance Code

- Section A Leadership
- Section B Effectiveness
- Section C Accountability
- Section D Remuneration
- Section E Relations with Shareholders

Exam focus

There is no requirement under the syllabu to know the detail of the UK Corporate Governance Code. It is, however, a good model of best practice requirements.

Developing governance codes

hapter

3

The board of directors

In this chapter

- Board of directors – roles and responsibilities.
- Board structures.
- Composition of the board.
- Purposes, roles and responsibilities of NEDs.
- Chairman and chief executive – roles and responsibilities.
- Induction and CPD.
- Performance evaluation.
- Rights and duties – all directors.
- Board committees – why have them?
- Nominations committee.

Board of directors – roles and responsibilities

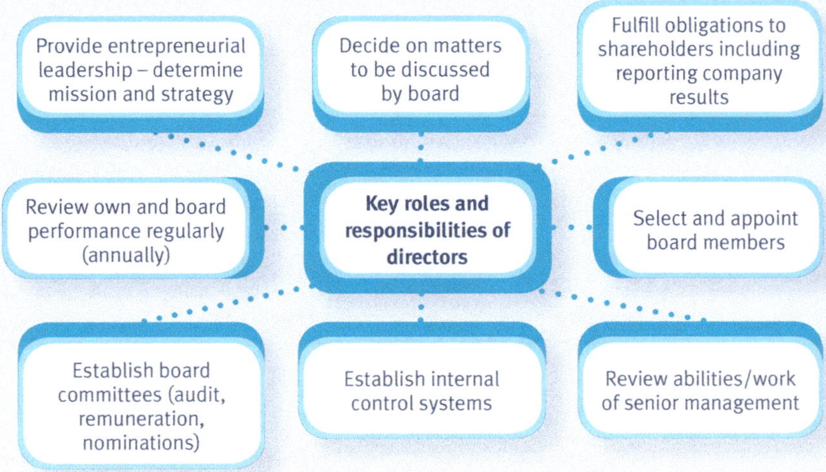

Board structures

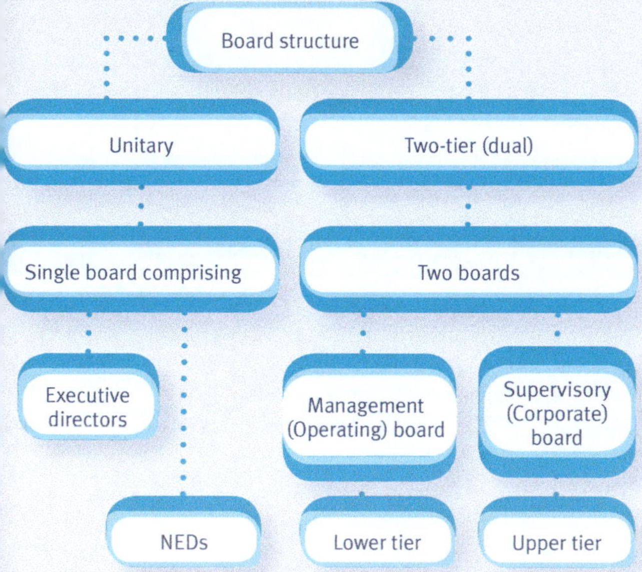

- Two-tier boards common where workers, banks etc. have more involvement with running of company
- Unitary boards common where shareholders are main stakeholders company considers – hence NEDs on board to promote shareholder interest

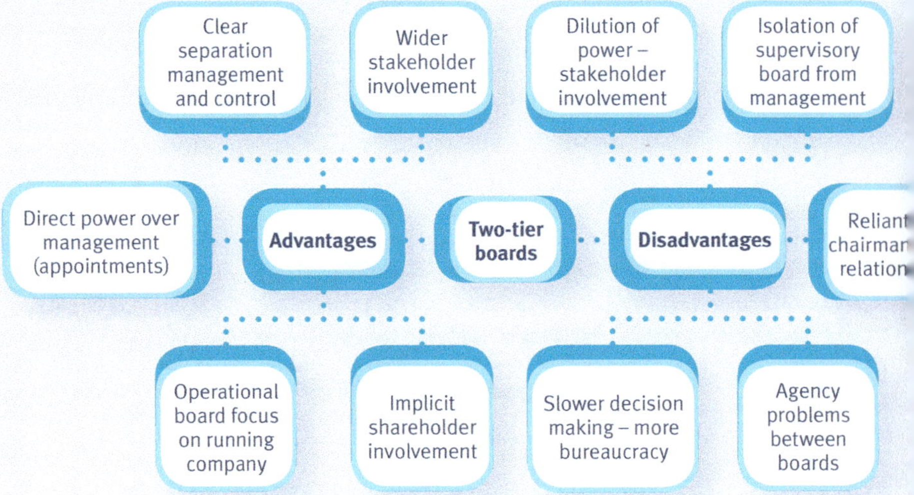
Clear separation management and control
Wider stakeholder involvement
Dilution of power – stakeholder involvement
Isolation of supervisory board from management
Direct power over management (appointments)
Advantages
Two-tier boards
Disadvantages
Operational board focus on running company
Implicit shareholder involvement
Slower decision making – more bureaucracy
Agency problems between boards

Exam focus

Board structures is an important area. You will need to be able to argue in favour of, or against, either unitary or two-tier boards.

Board diversity

The concept of diversity encompasses acceptance and respect.

It means understanding that each individual is unique, and recognising our individual differences.

These can be along the dimensions of:

- race
- ethnicity
- gender
- sexual orientation
- socioeconomic status
- age
- physical ability
- religious beliefs
- political beliefs or other ideologies.

Composition of the board

- Link between shareholders and managers – monitors the latter.
- Is the elected representative of the owners – must safeguard company assets for the owners.

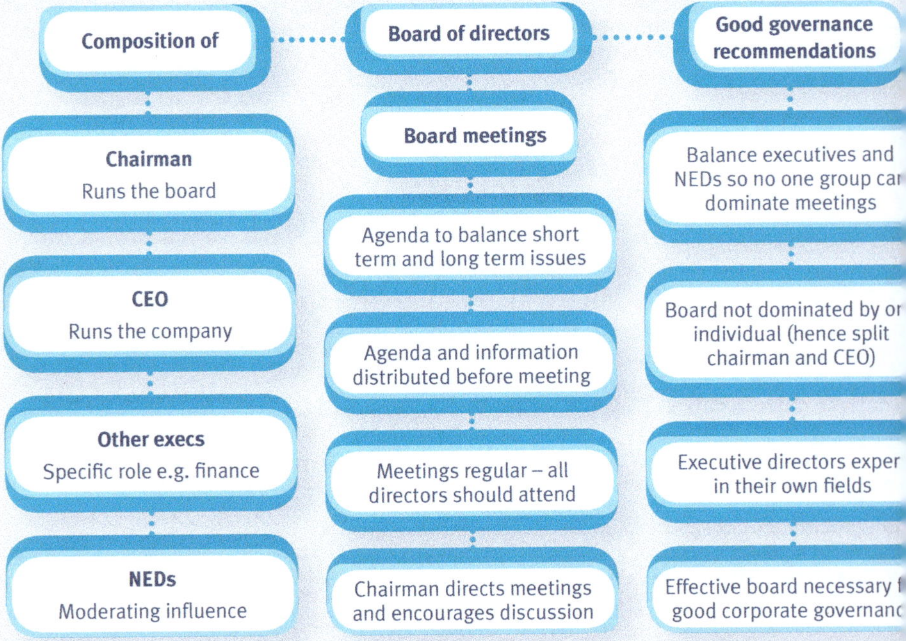
Composition of
Board of directors
Good governance recommendations
Chairman
Runs the board
CEO
Runs the company
Other execs
Specific role e.g. finance
NEDs
Moderating influence
Board meetings
Agenda to balance short term and long term issues
Agenda and information distributed before meeting
Meetings regular – all directors should attend
Chairman directs meetings and encourages discussion
Balance executives and NEDs so no one group ca
dominate meetings
Board not dominated by o
individual (hence split chairman and CEO)
Executive directors expe
in their own fields
Effective board necessary
good corporate governan

Purposes, roles and responsibilities of NEDs

- NED = director appointed to a non-executive role
- Must be independent of company to ensure role carried out correctly.

Main roles of NEDs

- Strategy – challenge and offer advice on company strategy
- Scrutinising – hold executive directors to account and review their decisions
- Risk – ensure adequate system of internal control and risk management
- People – appoint and decide remuneration of executive directors, and consider contractual and disciplinary issues.

Independence threats to NEDs

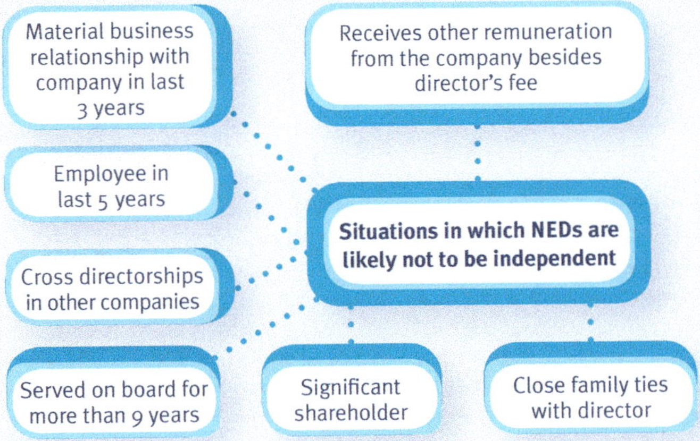

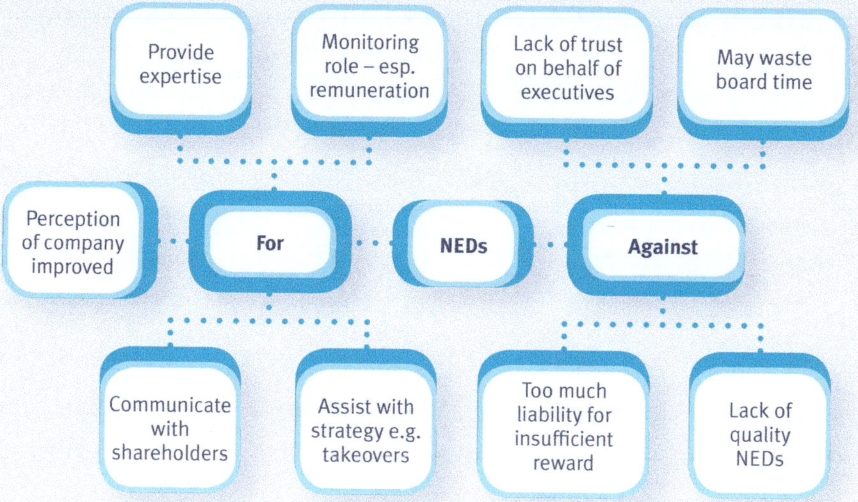
Provide expertise
Monitoring role – esp. remuneration
Lack of trust on behalf of executives
May waste board time
Perception of company improved
For
NEDs
Against
Communicate with shareholders
Assist with strategy e.g. takeovers
Too much liability for insufficient reward
Lack of quality NEDs

Chairman and chief executive – roles and responsibilities

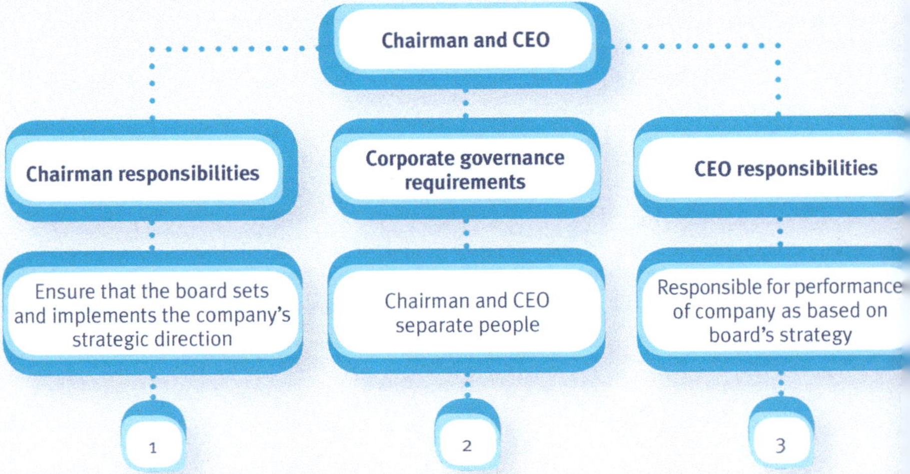

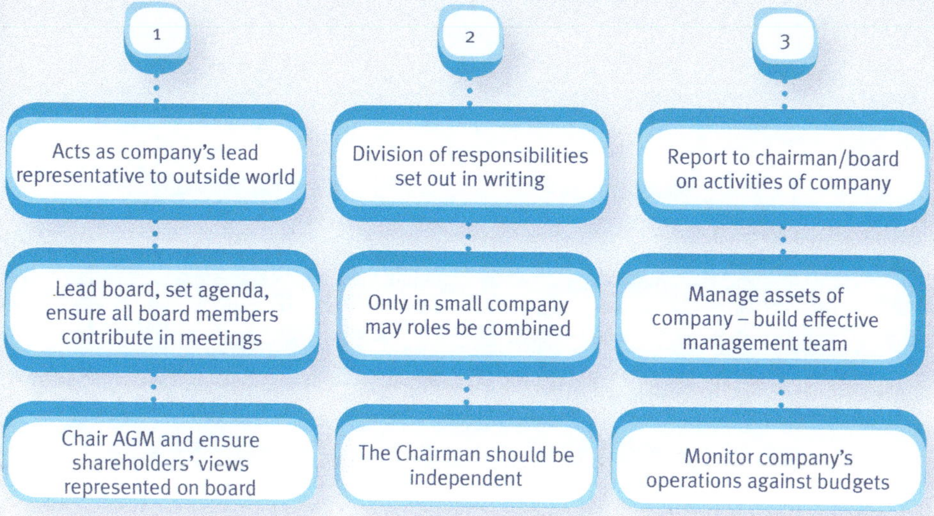
1
Acts as company's lead representative to outside world
Lead board, set agenda, ensure all board members contribute in meetings
Chair AGM and ensure shareholders' views represented on board
2
Division of responsibilities set out in writing
Only in small company may roles be combined
The Chairman should be independent
3
Report to chairman/board on activities of company
Manage assets of company – build effective management team
Monitor company's operations against budgets

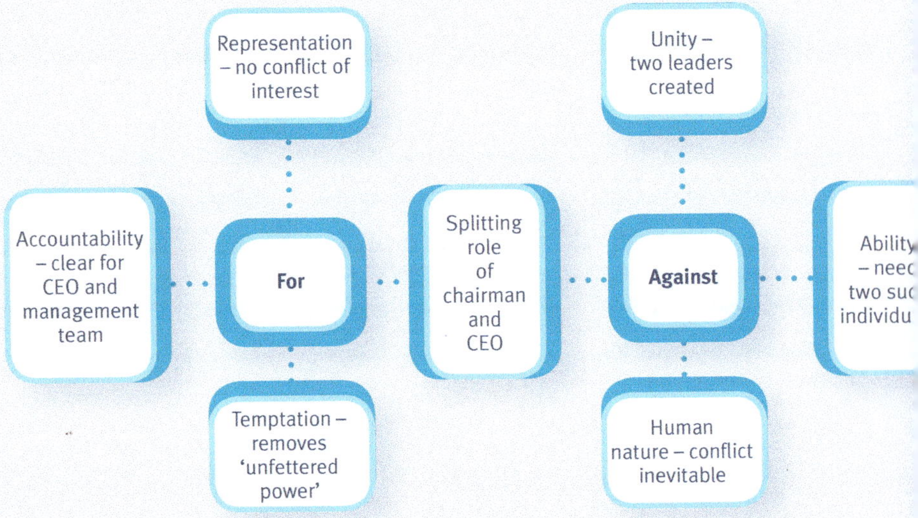
Representation – no conflict of interest
Unity – two leaders created
Accountability – clear for CEO and management team
For
Splitting role of chairman and CEO
Against
Ability – need two suc individu
Temptation – removes 'unfettered power'
Human nature – conflict inevitable

Induction and CPD

<table>
<tr><th>Induction</th><th>CPD</th></tr>
<tr><td>• Aims to provide director with knowledge of company and board strategy and other directors and employees.</td><td rowspan="2">• Aims to enhance the abilities of directors on a regular basis.
• Deciding appropriate CPD for each director: primary responsibility of the chairman.
• CPD also improves board effectiveness and meets personal development needs of directors.</td></tr>
<tr><td>• Major aspects include:
– Organisation's norms, values and culture
– Practical procedural duties and company policies
– Nature of the company
– Establishing relationships with colleagues.</td></tr>
</table>

Performance evaluation

- Carried out in three areas – as shown right
- Carried out annually – led by chairman (and NEDs to review chairman performance)
- Mixture of self-appraisal and discussion at board meetings
- Performance monitored against specific targets for each director
- Recommended to use external third party to ensure objectivity

Method of determining how well the board has worke directed company in last year

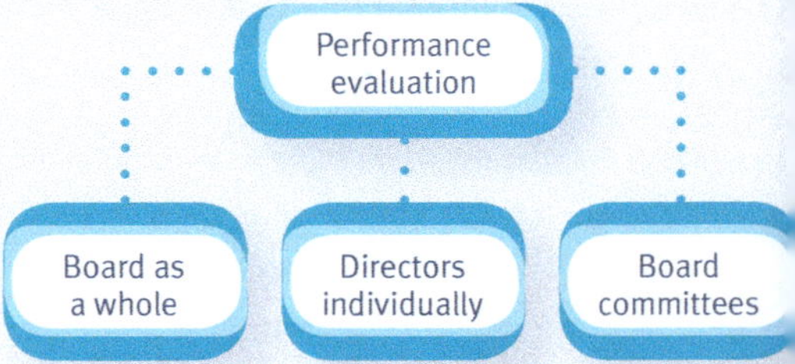

Rights and duties – all directors

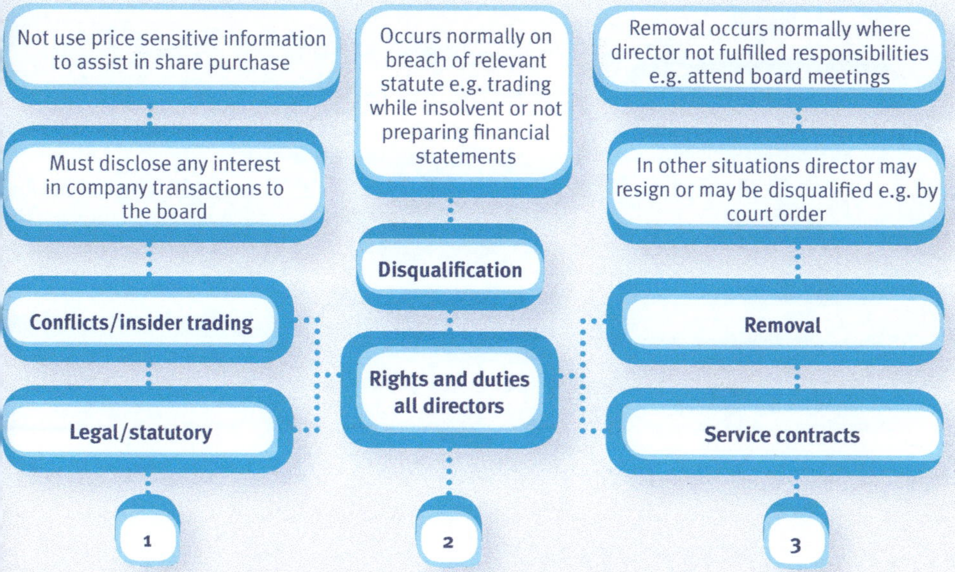

1

Act in good faith

- treating all shareholders equally
- declaring conflicts of interest
- not making personal profit

In UK, follow provisions of Companies Acts 1985 and 2006

2

Appointment and retirement

Appointed by nominations committee

Re-elected regularly – 3 year term maximum (All directors of FTSE 350 Companies should be subject to Annual election)

3

Covers conditions of employment including remuneration, duties etc.

Notice or contract period to be normally one year or less

Board committees – why have them?

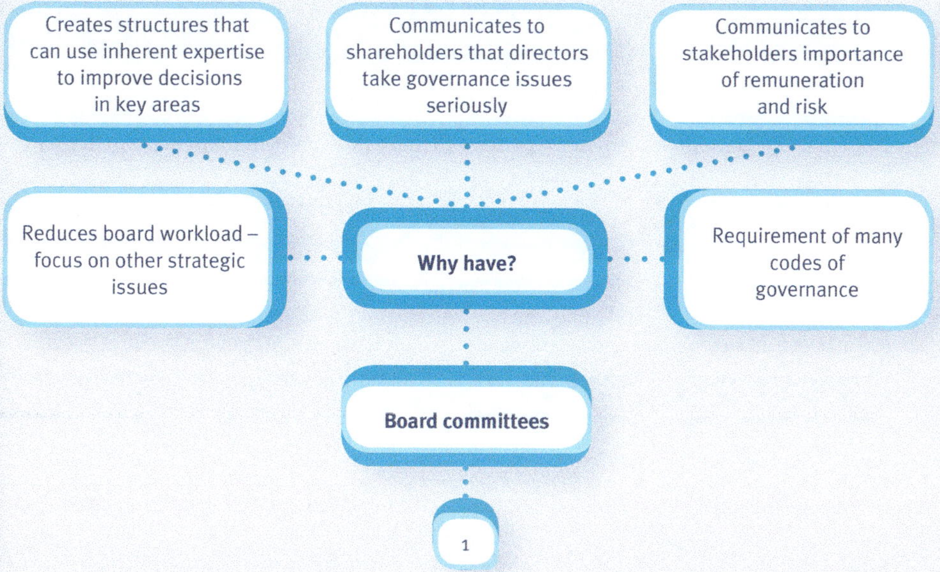

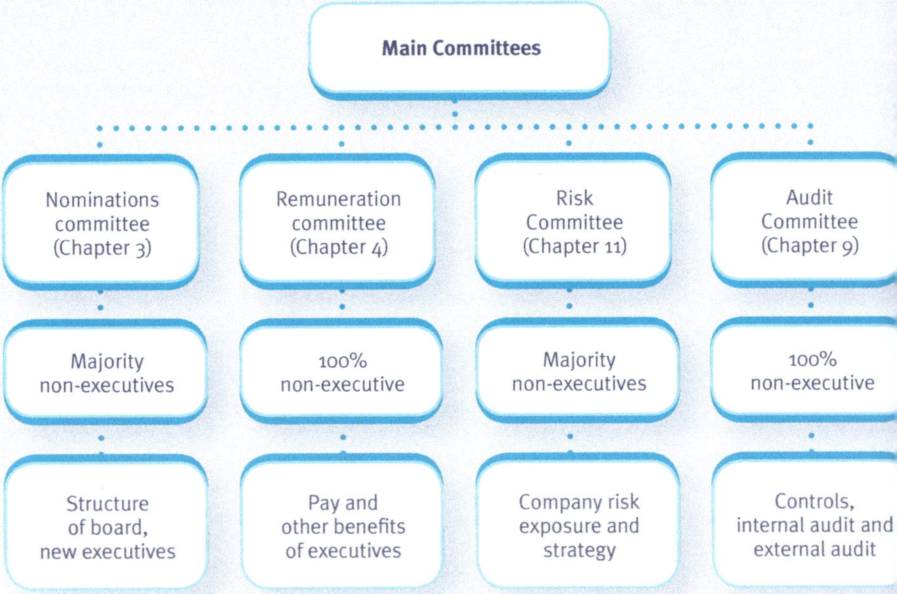
Main Committees
Nominations committee (Chapter 3)
Remuneration committee (Chapter 4)
Risk Committee (Chapter 11)
Audit Committee (Chapter 9)
Majority non-executives
100% non-executive
Majority non-executives
100% non-executive
Structure of board, new executives
Pay and other benefits of executives
Company risk exposure and strategy
Controls, internal audit and external audit

Nominations committee

The UK Corporate Governance Code requires that there should be a formal, rigorous and transparent procedure for the appointment of new directors to the board.

Exam focus

Recent P1 questions on this topic include:

Topic	Pilot	D07	J08	D08	J09	D09	J10	D10	J11	D11	J12	D12	J13	D13	J14	D
Board structure	Q1					Q2	Q4					Q2				
NEDs	Q1, SPQ3	Q1		Q2		Q1		Q3			Q2		Q4			
Chairman/ CEO		Q3			Q3	Q2			Q1	Q2						
Rights and duties					Q3											
Induction and CPD						Q2					Q4					
Nominations committee			Q3											Q4		

*SP refers to supplementary pilot question paper

chapter

4

Directors' remuneration

In this chapter

- Remuneration committee.
- Directors' remuneration.
- Remuneration – components and considerations.
- Directors' remuneration – other issues.

Remuneration committee

The role is to have an appropriate reward policy that attracts, retains and motivates directors to achieve the long-term interests of shareholders.

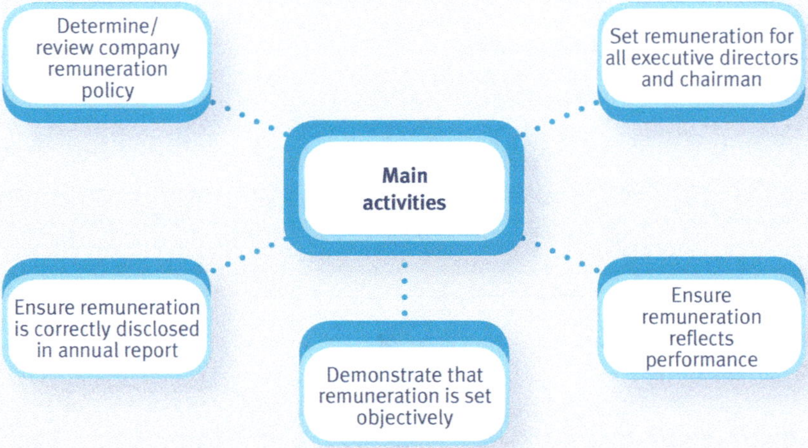

Directors' remuneration

Remuneration = payment received for services or employment.

- Remuneration committee sets remuneration for executive directors.
- NED remuneration consists of basic salary only.
- NED remuneration is set by board and shareholders.

Exam focus

Directors' remuneration is a highly topical subject, and is popular in examination questions. Be prepared to discuss the appropriateness of a given package, and how it could be improved. Always emphasise inclusion of a performance-related element in your answers.

Remuneration – components and considerations

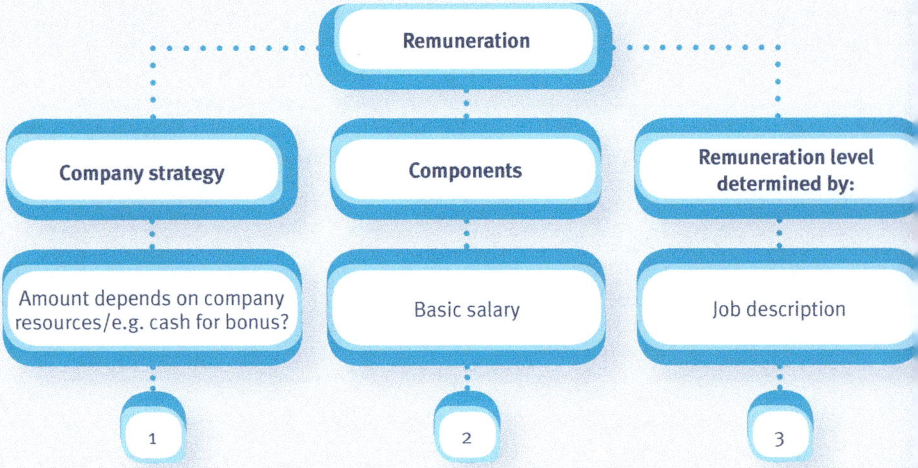

1

Judge where to position remuneration compared to other companies

Be aware of remuneration levels in comparable companies

Be aware of pay and conditions throughout the company

2

Performance related pay – linked to company success – short-term bonus – share options

Pension contributions

Benefits in kind

3

Not too small – could lead to lack of motivation/ underachievement

Not too easily earned to ensure that directors strive to improve performance

Significant proportion based on performance related elements

To attract and possibly motivate if increase with performance

Directors' remuneration – other issues

Legal	Ensure that in event of early termination amount of compensation is clear – and not excessive. Avoid rewarding poor performance.
Ethical	Directors encouraged to consider ethical impacts of company actions – may be element in employment contract/remuneration levels.
Competitive	Remuneration policy should be sufficient to attract and motivate directors – but seen to be excessive.
Regulatory	Ensure comply with legislation (e.g. directors remuneration regulations in UK). Additional regulation (e.g. Sarbanes-Oxley) has also led to increases in remuneration levels.

Exam focus

Recent P1 questions on this topic include:

Topic	Pilot	D07	J08	D08	J09	D09	J10	D10	J11	D11	J12	D12	J13	D13	J14	D14
Remuneration committee	Q2						Q2			Q3						
Remuneration package	Q2	Q2			Q3		Q2			Q3			Q4			

*SP refers to supplementary pilot question paper

ıapter

5

Relations with shareholders and disclosure

In this chapter

- Institutional investors.
- Institutional shareholder intervention.
- General meetings.
- Disclosure.
- Mandatory vs voluntary disclosure.

Institutional investors

Types of investors	Potential problems
• Pension funds • Life assurance companies • Unit trusts • Investment trusts	• Fund managers view: investments made for financial gain, not interested in governance, short-termism • Skills: many fund managers part-time, lack skills for responsible investment • Shareholder activism: some investors taking role of shareholder more seriously since increase in corporate governance requireme

nstitutional shareholder intervention

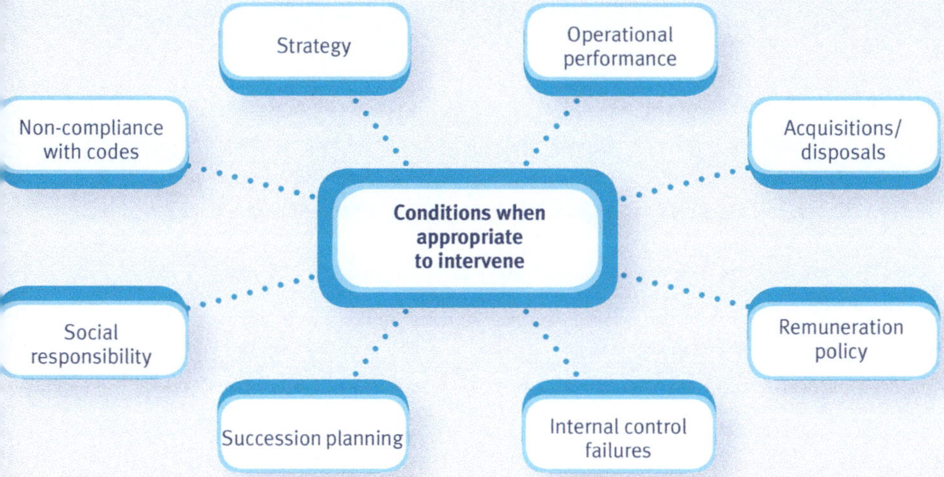

General meetings

Meeting of shareholders to discuss business relating to company. Proxy voting ensures that shareholders unable to attend can still voice opinions.

Two types:

Annual General Meeting (AGM)	Extra-ordinary General Meeting (EGM)
• Held annually: statutory requirement • Minimum 20 days notice • All shareholders can attend/vote • Normal business includes presentation of accounts/appointment directors and auditors	• Held as required: no legal obligation • Minimum 14 days notice • All shareholders can attend/vote • No set business – agenda established according to need

Disclosure

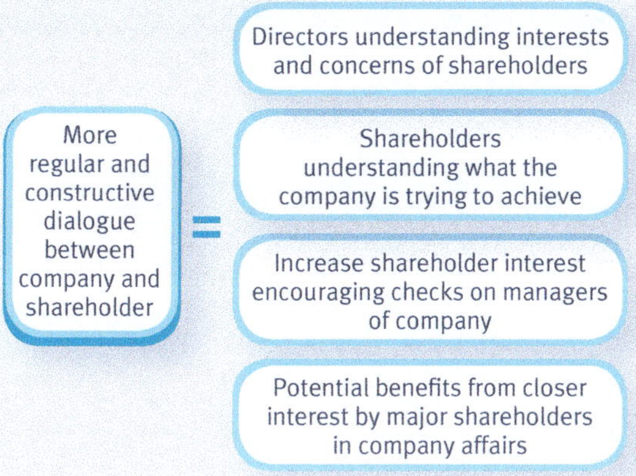
More regular and constructive dialogue between company and shareholder
=
Directors understanding interests and concerns of shareholders
Shareholders understanding what the company is trying to achieve
Increase shareholder interest encouraging checks on managers of company
Potential benefits from closer interest by major shareholders in company affairs

Mandatory vs voluntary disclosure

- Mandatory: information required to comply with laws or regulations.
- Voluntary: additional information which a company discloses should it choose to do so.

Exam focus

You will need to be able to discuss exam of types and methods of disclosure. Don forget that CSR reporting can be conside as enhancing voluntary disclosure.

Strong disclosure regime can help to attract capital and maintain confidence in company

Shareholders and potential investors require access to regular, reliable, comparable information for decision making

May be made to promote the company in a positive light, and act as a marketing tool

Weak disclosure and non-transparent practices can contribute to unethical behaviour and loss of market integrity

Voluntary disclosures made by the company when no legal obligation to do so exists

Helps improve public understanding of the structure, activities, corporate policies and performance

Exam focus

Recent P1 questions on this topic include:

Topic	Pilot	D07	J08	D08	J09	D09	J10	D10	J11	D11	J12	D12	J13	D13	J14
Institutional shareholders	SPQ3				Q1			Q1		Q1					Q1
Disclosure				Q1				Q2		Q1		Q2		Q2	Q2

*SP refers to supplementary pilot question paper

hapter 6

Corporate governance approaches

In this chapter

- Approaches to corporate governance.
- Sarbanes-Oxley (SOX).
- Organisation structure and governance.
- Corporate governance codes for multiple jurisdictions.

Approaches to corporate governance

Rules-based		Principles-based
• Instills the code into law with appropriate penalties for transgression.	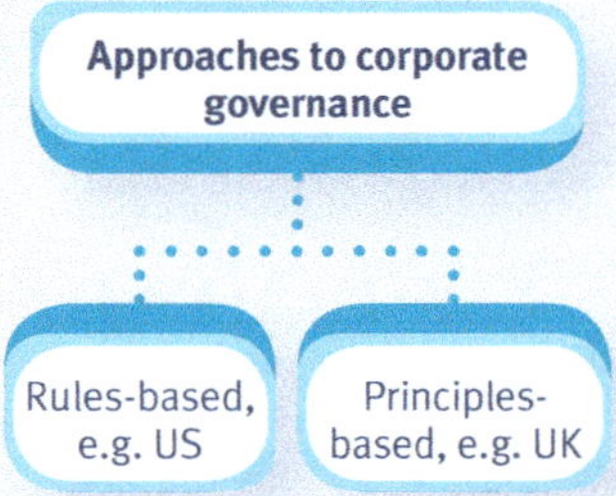	• Requires adherence to spirit rather than letter code. • Comply or explain why followed.

Exam focus

You will need to establish the type of governance regime a company is operating within at the of any governance question.

Be prepared to argue for or against either of these approaches (see next page).

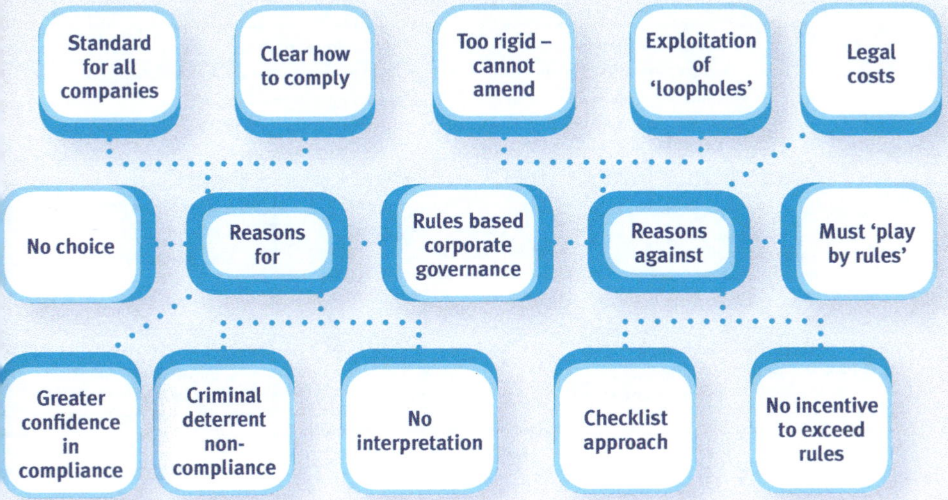
Standard for all companies
Clear how to comply
Too rigid – cannot amend
Exploitation of 'loopholes'
Legal costs
No choice
Reasons for
Rules based corporate governance
Reasons against
Must 'play by rules'
Greater confidence in compliance
Criminal deterrent non-compliance
No interpretation
Checklist approach
No incentive to exceed rules

Sarbanes-Oxley (SOX)

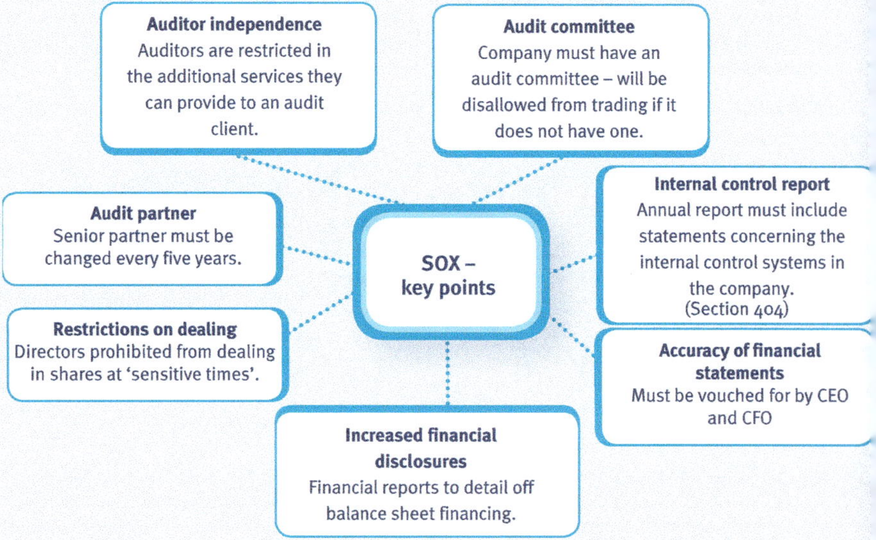

Negative reactions to SOX

- Audit fee costs.
- Onerous documentation.
- Reduced flexibility.
- Reduced risk taking.
- Limited impact on ability to stop corporate abuse.
- Legislation defines minimum only.

Organisation structure and governance

Business type	Family owned	Joint-stock
Governance objectives	• prevent dominance of any individual • protect rights of minority shareholders • provide structure for business ethics	• create relationship between shareholders and directors • ensure directors fairly remunera • ensure independence of auditor • ensure balance of power on boa of directors

Ownership	Inside	Outside
Description	Dominated/owned by inside shareholders	Owned by outside shareholders
Problems	Little separation of ownership and control Lack of minority shareholder protection	Big agency issues

Corporate governance codes for multiple jurisdictions

Codes are voluntary and not legally enforceable unless incorporated in the legal framework of individual countries

Code	Organisation for Economic Co-operation and Development (OECD)	International Corporate Governance Network (ICGN)
Who is?	Forum where market economies can exchange ideas/polices	Forum for parties interested in developing global corporate governance policies
Focus	Publicly traded companies – useful also for non-traded	Market traded securities – could apply to non-traded
Aim	Provide common basis for governance in all OECD countries	Produce governance standards that can be used in any jurisdiction
Governance principles	• Basis for effective corporate governance • Rights and equitable treatment of shareholders • Role of stakeholders • Disclosure and transparency • Responsibilities of the board	• Corporate objective – shareholder return • Disclosure and transparency • Audit • Shareholder responsibilities • Director remuneration • Corporate citizenship

Exam focus

Recent P1 questions on this topic include:

Topic	Pilot	D07	J08	D08	J09	D09	J10	D10	J11	D11	J12	D12	J13	D13	J14
Rules/ principles approach	SPQ3		Q4				Q3			Q2		Q2		Q2	
Multiple jurisdiction		Q3													

*SP refers to supplementary pilot question paper

hapter

7

Corporate social responsibility and corporate governance

In this chapter

- Social responsibility.
- Social responsiveness.
- Stakeholder theory.
- Classifications of stakeholders.
- Managing stakeholder relations.
- Organisational motivation regarding stakeholders.
- The organisation as a corporate citizen.
- Shareholder ownership, property and responsibilities.

Social responsibility

- Corporation is separate legal entity therefore has responsibilities to others.
- Work on principle of 'enlightened self-interest' – if make positive contribution to society this also benefits company.
- Corporate social responsiblity (CSR) refers to organisations considering and managing their impact on a variety of stakeholders.

Exam focus

This is an area that can appear in many topics within this exam. It can be seen with stakeholders, environmental issues corporate governance theory.

Developing a CSR strategy

To achieve company goals strategies are needed to ensure that everyone in the organization is headed in the right direction at the right time and that resources are available to support these goals when and where required.

A suggested approach to develop and pursue CSR strategy is as follows:

- The board, must make an authentic, firm, and public commitment to CSR.
- Determine the critical business objectives and priorities of the company.
- Develop a CSR strategy that will contribute to the achievement of those objectives.
- Align CSR strategy with the firm's core competencies.
- Integrate CSR into the culture, governance and strategy development of the company.
- Develop key performance indicators to measure the impact of their CSR strategies.

Corporate social responsibility (Carroll)

- 'Encompasses the economic, legal, ethical and philanthropic expectations placed on organisations by society at a given point in time'.

True social responsibility means meeting all four layers ("expectations" in Carroll's definition).

Layer	Name	Explanation
1	Economic	Reasonable return to shareholders Employee safety, fair pay Provide customers with quality products at fair price
2	Legal	Follow legislation as a minimum for CSR
3	Ethical	Do what is right, just and fair – more than just follow law
4	Philanthropic	Discretionary behaviour to improve the life of others including charitab donations and sponsoring arts

Social responsiveness

This refers to the capacity of the corporation to respond to social pressure, and the manner in which it does so.

Carroll suggested four strategies:

Strategy	**Explanation**
Reaction	The corporation denies any responsibility for social issues.
Defence	The corporation admits responsibility but fights it.
Accommodation	The corporation accepts responsibility and does what is demanded of it.
Proaction	The corporation seeks to go beyond industry norms.

Stakeholder theory

Definition

Stakeholder = any person or group that can affect or be affected by the policies or activities of an organisation.

Who are stakeholders?

- The capitalist view 'Customers, suppliers, shareholders and employees'.
- Stakeholder model view adds 'Government, civil society and competitors'.

Stakeholder claims = demands that the stakeholder makes of an organisation.

Exam focus

The examiner has written two articles, published in Student Accountant, about stakeholders. Stakeholders commonly appear in the compulsory question.

Classifications of stakeholders

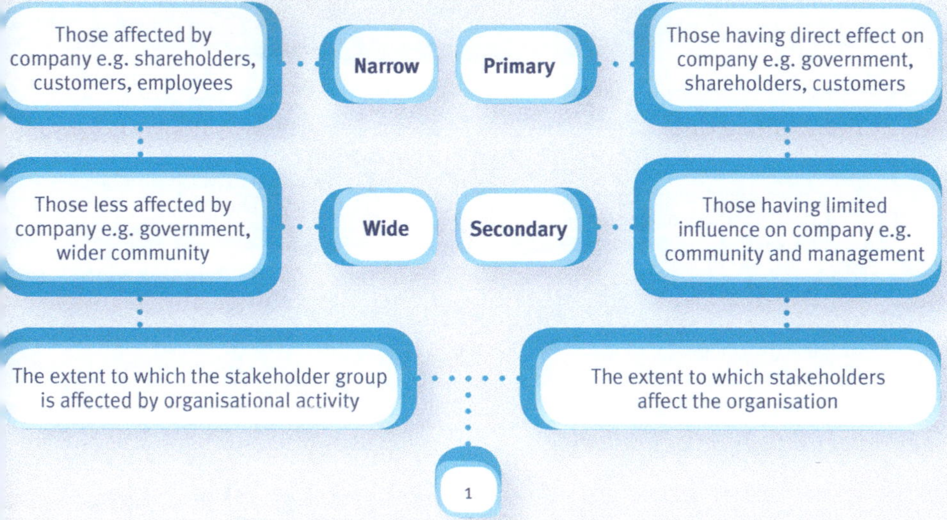

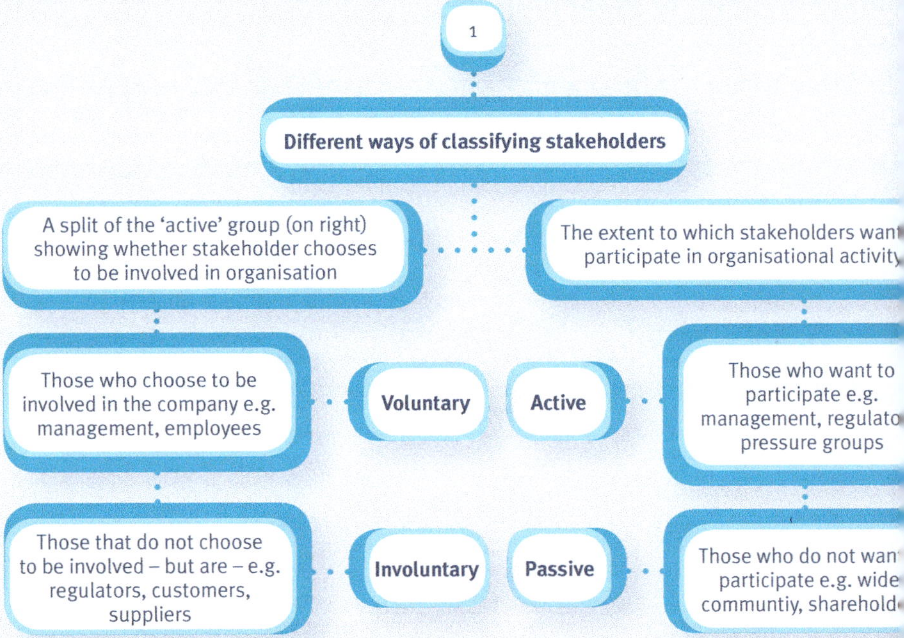
1
Different ways of classifying stakeholders
A split of the 'active' group (on right) showing whether stakeholder chooses to be involved in organisation
The extent to which stakeholders wan participate in organisational activit
Those who choose to be involved in the company e.g. management, employees
Voluntary
Active
Those who want to participate e.g. management, regulato pressure groups
Those that do not choose to be involved – but are – e.g. regulators, customers, suppliers
Involuntary
Passive
Those who do not wan participate e.g. wide communtiy, sharehold

Managing stakeholder relations

Mendelow's stakeholder mapping matrix

- Classifies stakeholders according to their level of power and interest in the organisation.
- Matrix used to determine company's action regarding each group.
- Company focus on key players, then those to keep satisfied to ensure they do not become key players.

Power	Level of interest: Low	Level of interest: High
Low	Minimal effort	Keep informed
High	Keep satisfied	Key players

Organisational motivation regarding stakeholders

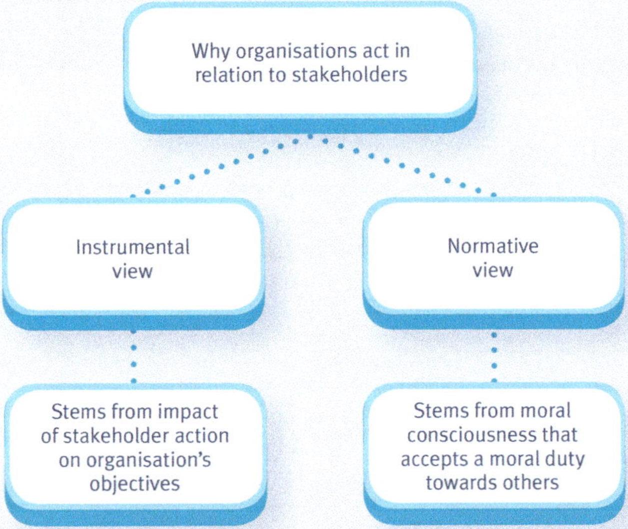

The organisation as a corporate citizen

Corporate citizen = expanded view of corporation in society. Implies corporate accountability.

Corporate accountability = whether the organisation is in some way answerable for the consequences of its actions beyond its relationship with shareholders.

Reasons for viewing company as corporate citizen

Government failure

- Government may be too slow to legislate against risks with new products and services.
- Other influences e.g. lack of political will, actions of pressure groups etc. also impede government action.
- Company must therefore take responsibility for safety of products/services.

Corporate power

- Over time, companies have tended to gain more power.
- E.g. decisions on where to locate workforce, privatisation of 'old' state monopolies.
- Companies should therefore use that power responsibly.

Shareholder ownership, property and responsibilities

Concepts applicable to shareholders:

Ownership	Responsibilities
• Means right to participate in the company – cannot 'own' company as it is a separate legal entity. • 'Reward' of ownership = dividend. Risk decreased by limited liability. • Shareholders, as owners of company, entitled to information on how company is performing. • Directors responsible for setting up/ maintaining communication channels with shareholders. • In many situations, disclosure is a requirement of good corporate governance.	• Democracy – ability to vote/influence company. • Activism – speak at general meeting. • Ethics – select investment opportunities company actions.

Exam focus

Recent P1 questions on this topic include:

Topic	Pilot	D07	J08	D08	J09	D09	J10	D10	J11	D11	J12	D12	J13	D13	J14	D14
Stakeholders	SPQ1	Q4	Q1		Q1		Q1				Q1	Q4				Q1
Normative/ instrumental	SPQ1															

*SP refers to supplementary pilot question paper

hapter

8

Internal control systems

In this chapter

- Board responsibilities.
- Internal control definitions.
- Sound control systems.
- Roles and responsibilities in risk management and internal control.
- Reviewing effectiveness of an internal control system (COSO).
- Information flows for management.
- Information quality.
- Information characteristics.

Board responsibilities

The board should maintain a sound system of internal control to safeguard shareholders' interests and company assets

Directors should implement a sound system of internal controls

This system should be reviewed on a regular basis (at least annually)

Internal control definitions

Definition

Controls attempt to ensure that risks are minimised.

Internal control system	=	whole network of systems in an organisation to provide reasonable assurance that organisational objectives will be achieved.
Internal management control	=	procedures and policies in place to ensure that company objectives are achieved.

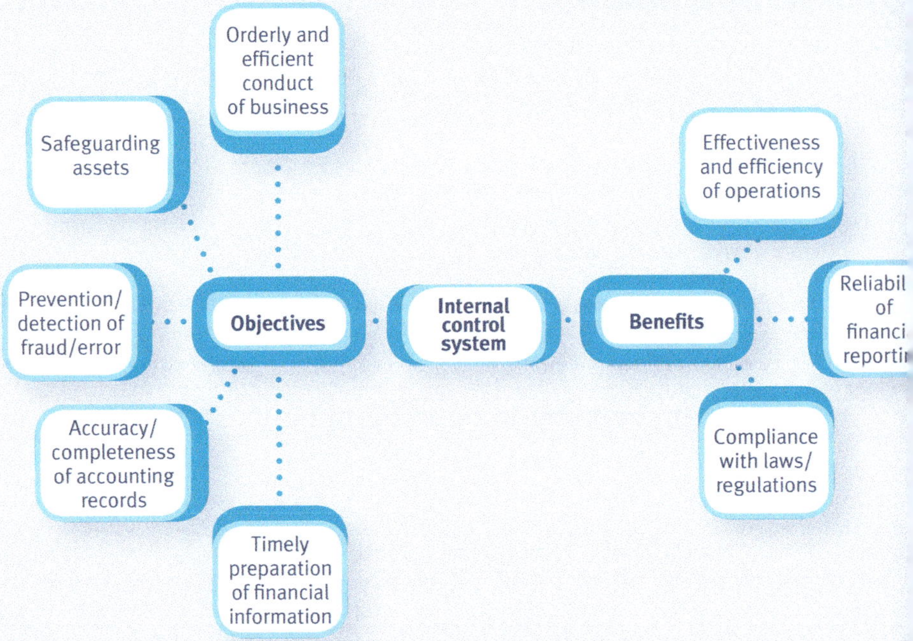
Orderly and efficient conduct of business
Safeguarding assets
Prevention/ detection of fraud/error
Objectives
Accuracy/ completeness of accounting records
Timely preparation of financial information
Internal control system
Benefits
Effectiveness and efficiency of operations
Compliance with laws/ regulations

Sound control systems

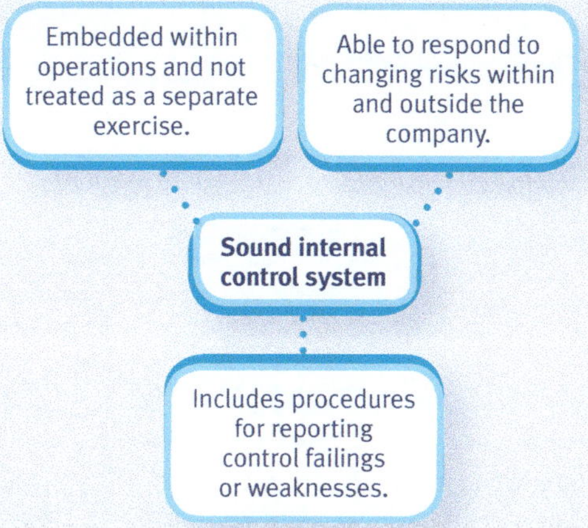

Exam focus

f the question requires you to discuss whether a particular system is ‘sound’ use the three eadings above. If it requires you to review, or discuss how auditors would review the effectiveness’ of a system refer to the COSO five elements that follow.

Roles and responsibilities in risk management and internal control

Many stakeholders involved – not just directors.

Role	**CEO**	**Board of directors**	**Risk committee**	**Executive management**
Responsibility	Ultimate responsibility for internal control system	• Ensuring adequacy and effectiveness of internal control system • Set corporate governance policy	Assists board in risk management obligations	Setting interna control policie and monitorin effectiveness c those system

Role	**Internal auditors**	**Heads of business units**	**All employees**	**External auditors**
Responsibility	• Evaluate the effectiveness of internal controls • Recommend improvements	Establish specific internal control procedures and policies for their units	Operating and adhering to internal control procedures	Advice on establishing and monitoring internal controls

Reviewing effectiveness of an internal control system (COSO)

Elements of an internal control system

COSO classification

1 Control environment

- 'Tone at the top' or the ethics and culture of the organisation. Set by management philosophy and style

2 Risk assessment

- Set objectives of organisation
- Then for each objective, identify and assess the risks affecting that objective
- Consider internal and external risks
- Distinguish between controllable and uncontrollable risks

3 Control activities

- Policies and procedures ensuring decisions and instructions of management carried out
- Occur at all levels in an organisation

4 Information & communication

- Communicate correct information to correct people so they can carry out their responsibilities
- Need quality information systems providing internal and external information

5 Monitoring

- Control system must be monitored – normally by internal audit

Information flows for management

Three management levels recognised in company.

Each level has responsibilities for internal controls and risk.

Information systems available to provide required information for each level.

Management level	Activity	Internal control responsibilities	Risk responsibilities
Strategic	Monitoring and controlling organisation as a whole	Reviewing internal control systems to ensure they are effective	Assess the risk outcomes of different decisions – also advised by the risk committee
1	2	3	4

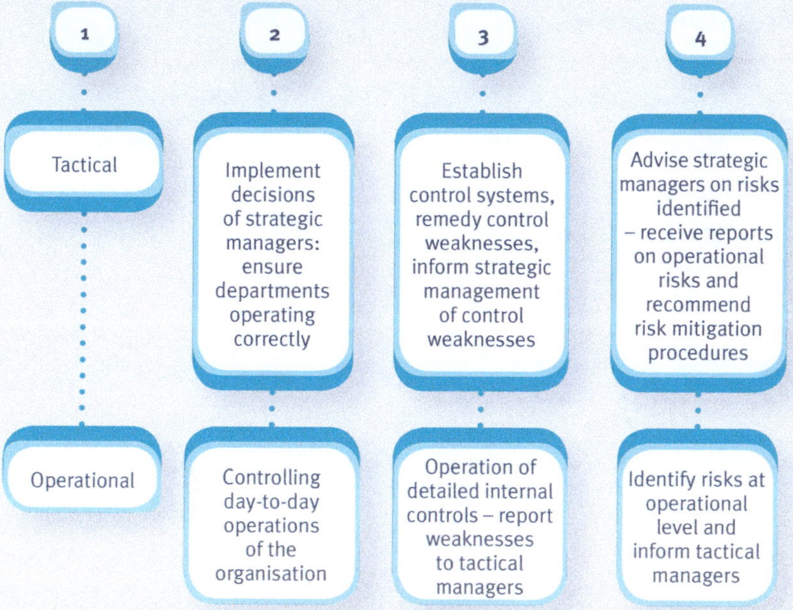
1
Tactical
Operational
2
Implement decisions of strategic managers: ensure departments operating correctly
Controlling day-to-day operations of the organisation
3
Establish control systems, remedy control weaknesses, inform strategic management of control weaknesses
Operation of detailed internal controls – report weaknesses to tactical managers
4
Advise strategic managers on risks identified – receive reports on operational risks and recommend risk mitigation procedures
Identify risks at operational level and inform tactical managers

Information quality

Information should meet the criteria of 'good' information:

- Accurate
- Complete
- Cost-beneficial
- User-targeted
- Relevant
- Authoritative
- Timely
- Easy to use

Exam focus

Questions in this area are likely to focus on the impact of poor quality information internal controls or risk management.

You may be required to recommend improvements to information received by managers.

Information characteristics

Key characteristics of information systems:

- company must have information to provide managers with all information they need
- information must be reliable, timely, accessible and provided in consistent format
- characteristics of information change depending on management level using information.

Characteristic	Strategic level	Operational level
Time period	Forecast	Historical
Timeliness	Delayed	Available now
Objectivity	Subjective	Objective
Quantifiability	Qualitative	Quantitative

Characteristic	Strategic level	Operational level
Accuracy	Approximate	Accurate
Certainty	Uncertain	Certain
Completeness	Partial	Complete
Detail	Little detail	Very detailed

Characteristics of tactical information lie between strategic and operational.

Exam focus

Recent P1 questions on this topic include:

Topic	Pilot	D07	J08	D08	J09	D09	J10	D10	J11	D11	J12	D12	J13	D13	J14	D14
Objectives of control systems				Q3			Q3				Q1					
Sound control systems	Q4												Q1 Q2			Q4
Control failure / improvements		Q1	Q1	Q3	Q1	Q1		Q1	Q1	Q1	Q1	Q3				
Information for management						Q1						Q3				

hapter

9

Audit and compliance

In this chapter

- Function and importance of internal audit.
- Factors affecting the need for internal audit.
- Organisational structure for internal audit.
- Auditor independence.
- Potential ethical threats.
- Audit committee.
- Audit committee and internal controls.
- Audit committee and internal audit.
- Audit committee and external auditors.
- Reporting on internal controls to shareholders.

Function and importance of internal audit

Definition

Internal audit = an independent appraisal activity established within an organisation as a service

Main roles/functions of internal audit:

Factors affecting the need for internal audit

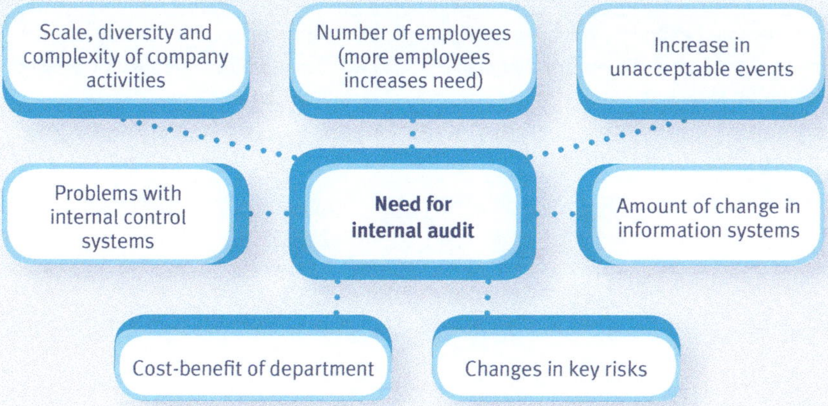

Organisational structure for internal audit:

• Chief internal auditor runs department • Chief internal auditor normally qualified (but no legal requirement for this)	• Reports to audit committee • Statutory requirement for listed compani in some countries (e.g. USA)

Auditor independence

Internal auditor independence necessary to ensure work carried out objectively.

Factors protecting independence

- Internal auditor independent of executive management.
- Chief internal auditor reports to audit committee.
- Chief internal auditor has access to Chairman.
- Audit committee approve appointment and termination of chief internal auditor.

Exam focus

You may be required to identify threats to independence in a scenario and suggest improvements.

The points given here form a good basis for your recommendations.

Potential ethical threats

= threats (real or perceived) to ability of auditor to provide independent opinion.

Apply to both internal and external audit.

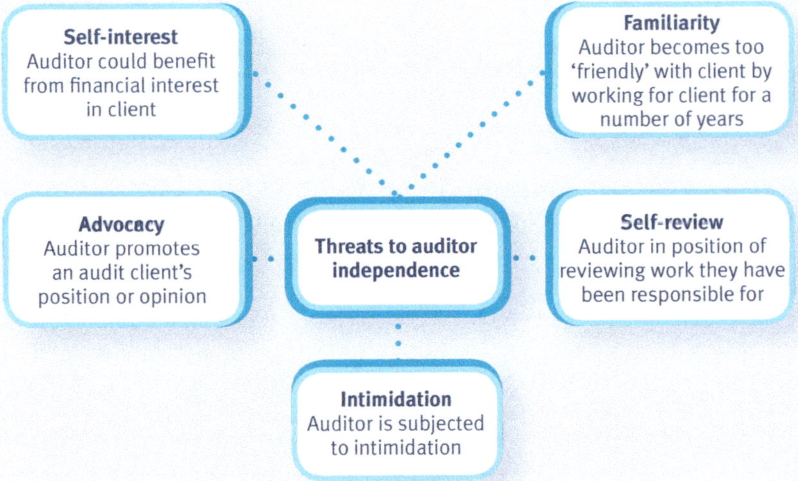

Audit committee

- Most of the board objectives relating to internal controls will be delegated to the audit committee.
- Consists entirely of NEDs – one with recent financial experience.

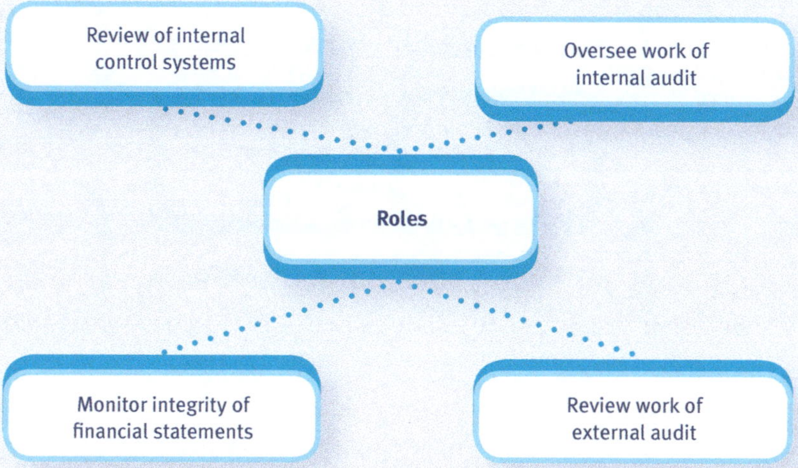

Audit committee and internal controls

Audit committee and internal audit

Audit committee responsible for overseeing work of internal audit function.

Audit committee and external auditors

Audit committee responsible for oversight of company relations with external auditors.

The UK Corporate Governance Code provides recommendations regarding the work of audit committee and company's external auditors:

Reporting on internal controls to shareholders

Important points regarding reporting to shareholders:

Exam focus

Recent P1 questions on this topic include:

Topic	Pilot	D07	J08	D08	J09	D09	J10	D10	J11	D11	J12	D12	J13	D13	J14	D
Internal audit	SPQ2			Q3			Q3						Q2	Q1		[illegible]
Auditor independence / threats			Q2		Q2											
Reporting on controls			Q4													

*SP refers to supplementary pilot question paper

hapter

10

Risk and the risk management process

In this chapter

- Risk.
- Risk management.
- Risk identification: Strategic and operational risks.
- Risk identification: Business risks.
- Risk identification: Sector-specific risks.
- Impact on stakeholders.
- Assessing risks.

Risk

Definition

A risk can be defined as an unrealised future loss arising from a present action or inaction.

Risks are the opportunities and dangers associated with uncertain future events.

Exam focus

Don't forget that risk has an upside potential as well as a downside.

Why incur risk?

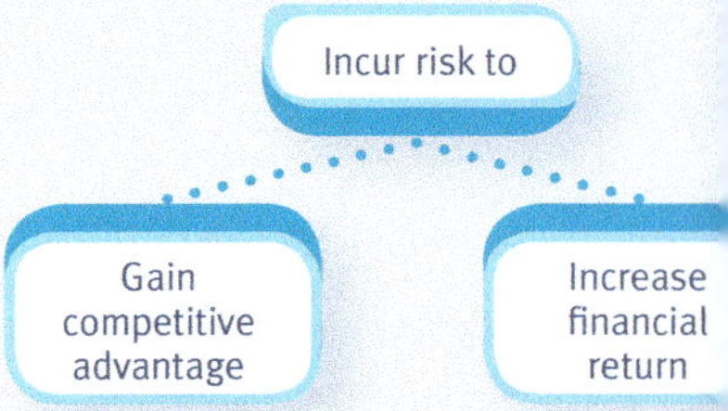

Why manage risk?

- Downside risks managed to identify risks and changes in existing risks.
- Upside risks identified to make best of opportunities.

Risk management

Definition

Risk management = process of reducing adverse consequences by reducing likelihood of event or its impact.

- Responsibility for risk management system rests with management.

The As Low As Reasonably Practicable Principle (ALARP)

- Expresses a point at which the cost of additional risk reduction would be grossly disproportionate to the benefits achieved.
- Usually applied to safety critical, high integrity systems e.g. oil rig.

Risk identification: Strategic and operational risks

Strategic risks	Operational risks
Risks arising from consequences of strategic decisions	Losses arising from business operations
Arise from strategic positioning of company in its environment	Arise from inadequate or failed internal processes
Risks include not enhancing old products and producing 'incorrect' new products	Risks include fraud, quality control failures a lack of production
Identified and assessed at senior management level. Managed by risk management strategy	Identified at operational level. Managed by internal control systems

Risk identification: Business risks

Definition

Business risks are strategic risks that threaten the health and survival of the whole business.

Risks per ACCA study guide

- **Market** – Sector trading in
- **Credit** – Inability to obtain funds required
- **Health and safety, environment** – Lack of compliance relevant laws
- **Financial**
  - Liquidity – Insufficient cash to run business
  - Gearing – High amounts of borrowing
- **Legal** – Does not follow relevant legislation
- **Technological** – Products not incorporate latest technology
- **Reputation** – 'Image' of company suffers
- **Business probity** – Company appears to act incorrectly
- **Derivatives** – Use of financial instruments to improve accounts

Exam focus

You need to be prepared to define any of these for two marks.

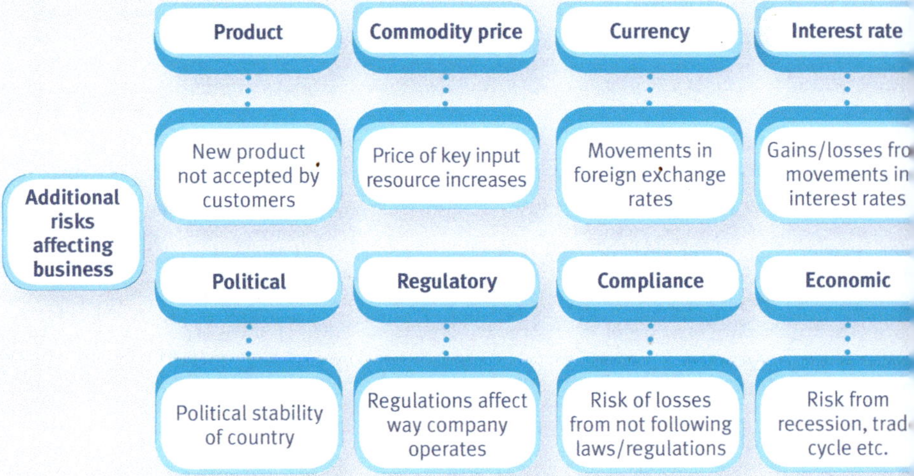
Additional risks affecting business
Product
New product not accepted by customers
Commodity price
Price of key input resource increases
Currency
Movements in foreign exchange rates
Interest rate
Gains/losses fro
movements in
interest rates
Political
Political stability of country
Regulatory
Regulations affect way company operates
Compliance
Risk of losses from not following laws/regulations
Economic
Risk from
recession, trad
cycle etc.

Risk identification: Sector-specific risks

Generic risks	Affect all business	Include interest rates, non-compliance company law
Specific risks	Affect individual business	How generic risk affects specific business

Impact on stakeholders

Business risks initially affect company – then affect stakeholders.

Impact depends on individual stakeholder type.

Related risk factors

- Related risks are risks that vary because of the presence of another risk.
- They do not exist independently.

CORRELATION BETWEEN RISK

POSITIVE CORRELATION

Both risks move in the same direction.

For example:

As the Environmental risk increases so does the reputational risk.

NEGATIVE CORRELATION

Each risk moves in an opposite direction.

For example:

As more money is spent on reducing the Environmental damage, therefore reducing the risk. There is an increase in the financial risk facing the company.

Assessing risks

Risks assessed using 'risk map'

- For each risk, shows impact on organisation and likelihood of risk occurring
- Allows risks to be prioritised
- Risks with high impact and likelihood of occurrence need urgent attention

Note on terminology:

- Impact = severity = hazard
- Likelihood = probability

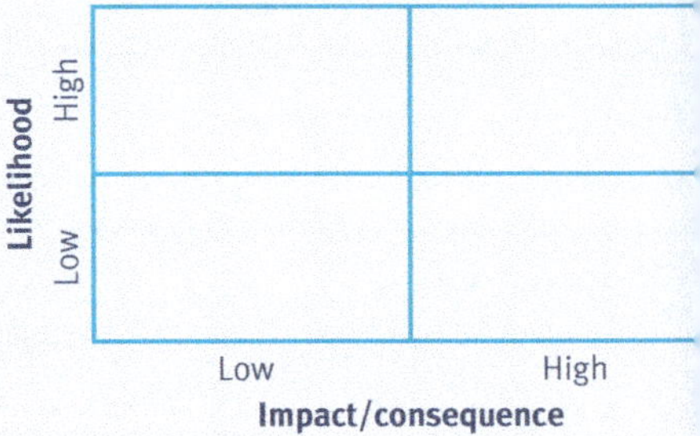

Dynamic nature of risk assessment

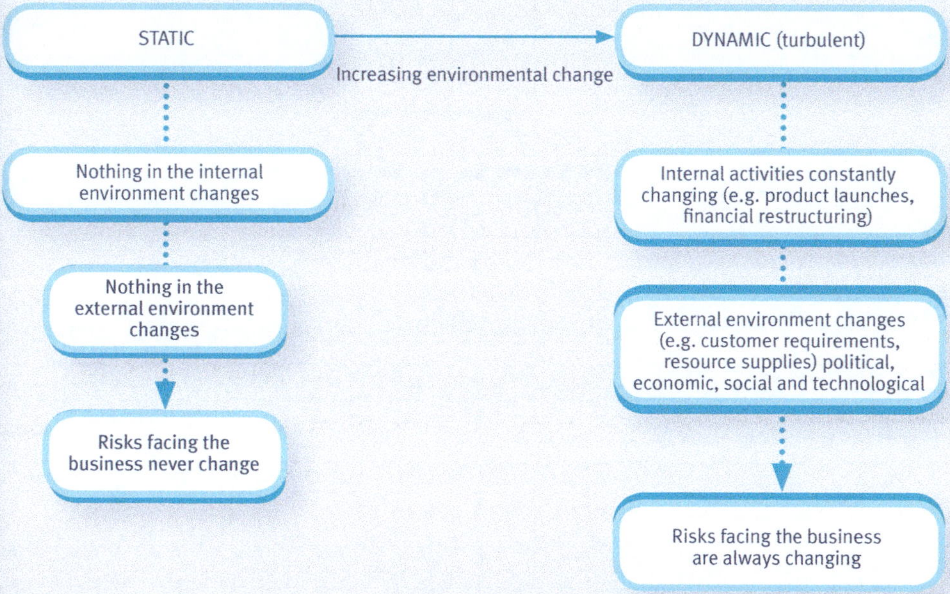

Risk perception

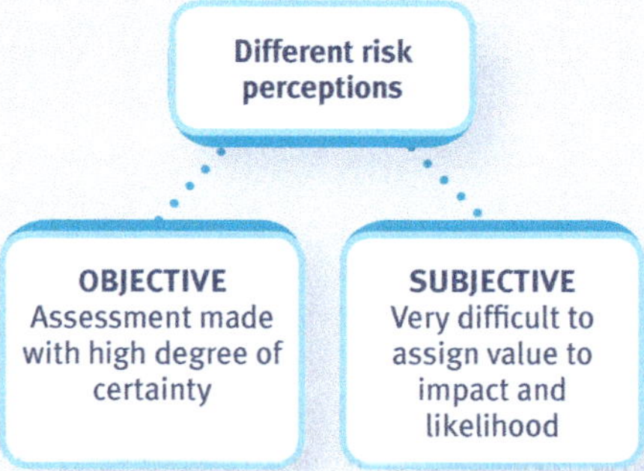

Exam focus

Recent P1 questions on this topic include:

Topic	Pilot	D07	J08	D08	J09	D09	J10	D10	J11	D11	J12	D12	J13	D13	J14	D
Risk identification/ assessment	Q1, Q4		Q1	Q1, Q3	Q4		Q1	Q2, Q4	Q1	Q3	Q1	Q1	Q1 Q3	Q1	Q2	

hapter

11

Controlling risk

In this chapter

- The role of the board.
- Risk attitude.
- Role of the risk manager and risk committee.
- Embedding risk in systems.
- Embedding risk in culture.
- Risk management.
- Risk mapping and risk management strategies.
- Risk auditing.
- External reporting.

The role of the board

Main role

- Considering risk at strategic level and defining organisation's appetite and approach to risk.

Other roles

- Setting risk appetite in terms of attitude and capacity.
- Communicating risk strategy to company.
- Monitoring risk management plans.
- Determining residual risk based on cost-benefit approach.

Framework for board consideration of risk

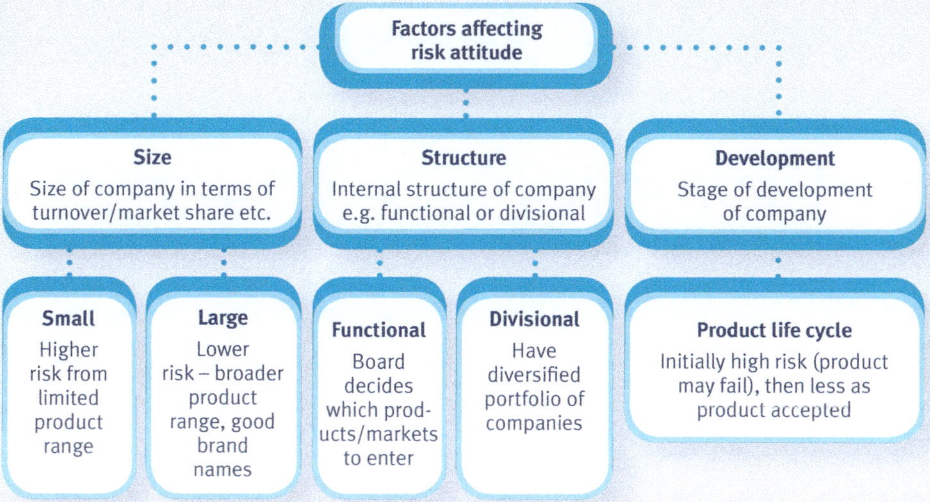
Factors affecting risk attitude
Size
Size of company in terms of turnover/market share etc.
Structure
Internal structure of company e.g. functional or divisional
Development
Stage of development of company
Small
Higher risk from limited product range
Large
Lower risk – broader product range, good brand names
Functional
Board decides which products/markets to enter
Divisional
Have diversified portfolio of companies
Product life cycle
Initially high risk (product may fail), then less as product accepted

Risk attitude

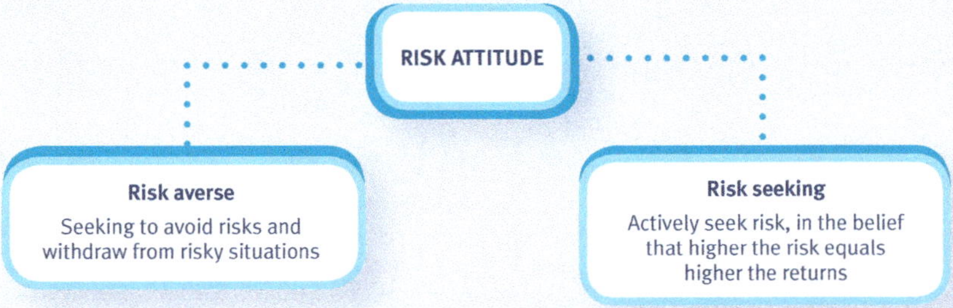

Role of the risk manager and risk commitee

Risk manager	Risk committee
Risk manager = member of risk management committee who reports direct to the board. Primary role = implementation of risk management policies.	Main aims: • Raise awareness of risk. • Ensure processes in place to identify, report and monitor risks. • Update company's risk profile.

Embedding risk in systems

- = ensuring risk management is included within control systems of an organisation
- Not a separate system – part of overall control system
- May be statutory requirement (USA) or code of practice (UK)

Process of embedding risk:

1. Identify controls already operating in organisation
2. Monitor controls to ensure they work
3. Improve/refine controls as required
4. Document how controls recorded and tested (e.g. performance metrics)

Embedding risk in culture

- Risk awareness is a capability of an organisation to be able to recognise risks when they arise, from whatever source they may come.

Embedding risk awareness

- Risk management being considered 'normal' for organisation therefore all employees follow risk management policies.
- Risk management culture starts at 'top' of company – provides open culture/better risk management.

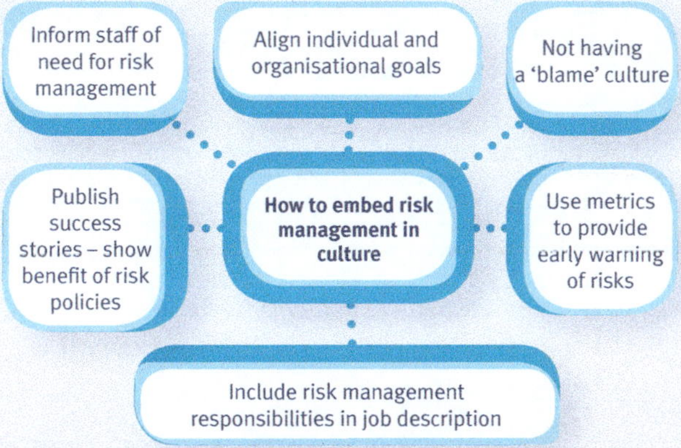

Risk management

- Strategies for managing risk = TARA (or SARA).

Transference (or sharing)	Transfer risk to third party e.g. use of insurance
Avoidance	Risk decreased to zero by avoiding risky areas e.g. withdrawing from busines area. However, risk may be unavoidable – so strategy has limited use
Reduction	Limit exposure to risk or decrease effects of risk should it crystallise
Acceptance	Accept risk may occur and choose to deal with consequences of risk if it does occur. Used where adverse impact of risk is minimal

Exam focus

- If question requires FOUR strategies to manage risk use the TARA model.

Risk mapping and risk management strategies

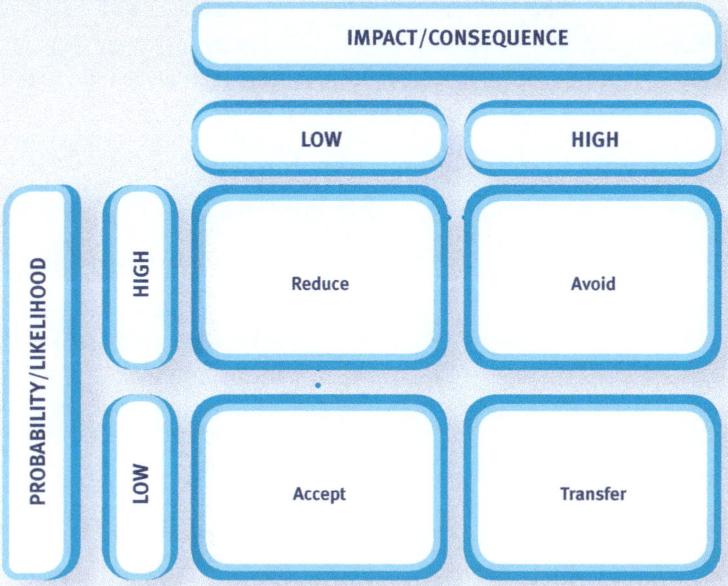

Further risk management strategies

- Risk avoidance = risk literally avoided.
- Risk retention = risk retained within organisation.

Diversifying/spreading risk

- Aim to reduce total risk.
- Can diversify operations
  - make different products or invest different countries.
- Works best where returns are negativ correlated.

Exam focus

If question requires suggestions for managing risks, and does not specify 'FO or any model like TARA, you will be requi to make practical suggestions of how to manage the given risks.

- Methods of portfolio management shown below:

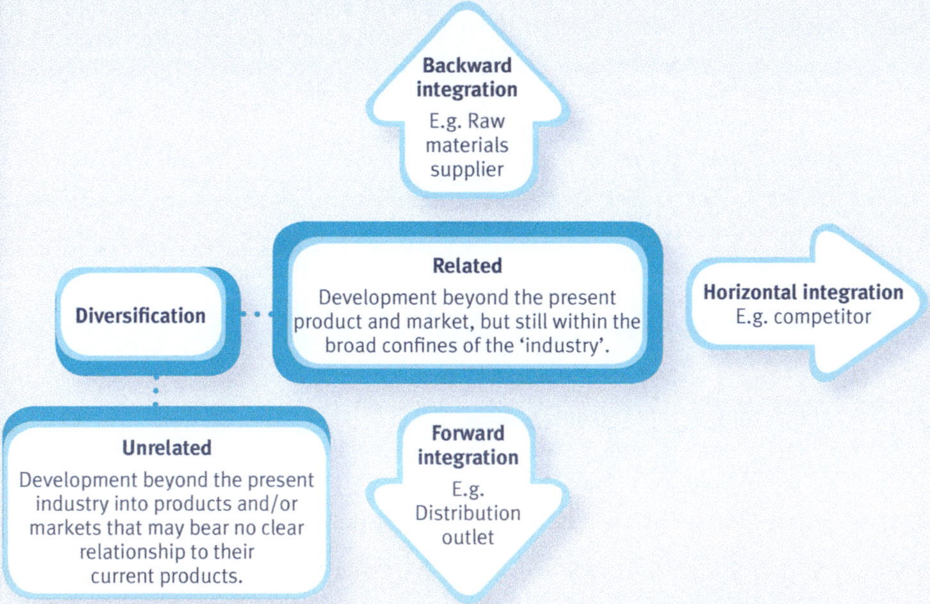

Risk auditing

Risk auditing

- = provision of independent view of risks and controls in organisation
- May be obligatory (e.g. Sarbanes-Oxley)
- Carried out by internal and/or external audit teams.

Exam focus

Risk audit is the topic of an article publis[h]
in Student Accountant written by your examiner.

External reporting

- External reporting of control risks relates to reporting to parties external to the company.
- Reporting required by statute, regulations or occasionally by third parties where company declines to report (e.g. money laundering, control failures in Sarbanes-Oxley).

Process of reporting is:

1 identify reporting situation

2 check compliance with legislation/ethical guidance

3 make report if required.

Exam focus

Recent P1 questions on this topic include:

Topic	Pilot	D07	J08	D08	J09	D09	J10	D10	J11	D11	J12	D12	J13	D13	J14
Risk committee	SP Q3			Q2							Q2				
Risk manager					Q4										
TARA		Q2		Q2					Q2			Q1		Q1	
Embedded risk		Q2				Q4		Q4							
Risk reporting audit						Q4									Q1

ıapter

12

Ethical theories

In this chapter

- Relativism and absolutism.
- Deontological and teleological approaches to ethics.
- Kohlberg's levels of cognitive moral development.
- Seven positions on social responsibility.
- Variables determining cultural context.
- Corporate and personal ethical stances.

Relativism and absolutism

Ethical theories

Relativism		**Absolutism**
Variety of beliefs and practices	**Definition**	One set of moral rights
Many sets: change over time	**Moral rules**	One set: always true
Depends on conditions at the time	**'Correctness' of action**	Depends on following rules

Absolutism = **dogmatic** approach: one truth to be imposed in all situations.

Relativism = **pragmatic** approach: attempt to find the 'best' solution in a particular ethical situat

Deontological and teleological approaches to ethics

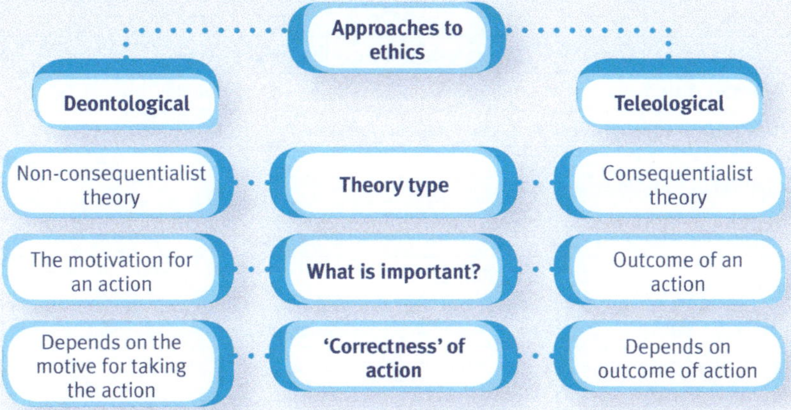

Deontological approach must satisfy three maxims:

	Maxim
1	**Consistency:** everyone must be able to follow the maxim
2	**Human dignity:** remember needs and expectations of all people
3	**Universality:** is action moral when viewed/known by others?

Approaches to **teleological** theory:

Egoism	Utilitarianism
Individuals pursue their own self-interests: society benefits because outcomes morally desirable for all.	Actions morally right where they provide the greatest good to the greatest number of people.
Companies pursue self-interest by producing high quality goods – society not harmed by poor quality goods and company makes profit.	Ensures good effects of actions outweigh ba effects – however can be subjective since measuring 'good' and 'bad' is difficult.

Kohlberg's levels of cognitive moral development

Level	Explanation	Stages
3: Post-conventional	Individual develops more autonomous decision making based on principle of rights and justice.	3.2: Universal ethical principles 3.1: Social contract and individual rights
2: Conventional	Individual does what is expected of them by others.	2.2: Social accord and system maintenance 2.1: Interpersonal accord and conformity
1: Pre-conventional	Individual shows concern with self-interest and external rewards and punishments.	1.2: Instrumental purpose and exchange 1.1: Obedience and punishment

- Attempts to show reasoning process used by individuals.
- Higher level reasoning shows more awareness of ethical issues in decision.
- Three levels each divided into two stages.

Seven positions on social responsibility

- Organisations should have some social responsibility.
- Social responsibility provides some accountability for organisation's actions.
- Corporate and Social Responsibility report (CSR) provides method of publishing that responsibility.
- 7 positions on responsibility (from Gray, Owens and Adams).

	Position	Comment
Pristine capitalist	World works as a liberal democracy: shareholder wealth maximisation is key	Needs of shareholders paramount. Little concept of CSR
Expedient	Social responsibility only valid when achieves interest of the business	Businesses need minimal ethical guidanc
Social contract	Companies only exist because society wants them – so companies must serve society	Actions of companies must serve the 'public interest'
Social ecologists	Businesses have a social and environmental footprint, and are responsible for minimising it	Economic systems need to change to place cost on resource use

Level	Position	Comment
Socialists	Capital should not be allowed to dominate social, economic and political life	Creation of 'things' should be secondary to individual well-being
Radical feminists	Businesses should have more 'feminine' characteristics such as equity, dialogue and compassion	Accounting and CSR systems flawed because do not 'value' compassion etc.
Deep ecologists	No business has a 'right' to resources – businesses lack environmental awareness	As a minimum, economic activity should be sustainable

Exam focus

Questions have asked you to 'argue from the perspective of' a given position. This may not be one that you personally agree with, but you will need to be comfortable with the implications of each of these views.

Variables determining cultural context

- Four factors affect ethical and cultural acts in different countries.
- US culture focuses on economic factors.
- European culture focuses on legal factors.

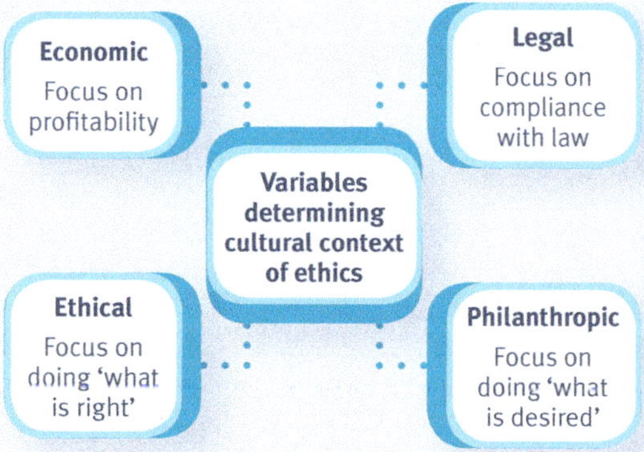

Variable	North American view	European view
Economic	Focus on profitability and interests of shareholders	Focus on actions of company – accept losses in short term to support social aims (retain employees rather than make redundant)
Legal	Government interference should be minimal – laws interfere with private liberty	Government is necessary to set and enforce laws
Ethical	Belief that organisations will normally act ethically	Organisations have ethical responsibilities and must follow those responsibilities
Philanthropic	Philanthropic acts expected from both companies and individuals	Regulatory systems provide all requirements – less expectation of philanthropic acts

Corporate and personal ethical stances

Theory	Explains	Corporate stance	Individual stance
Short term shareholder interest	Shareholder requirements in the short term	Provide adequate return to shareholders	Require annual return on investment (dividend)
Long term shareholder interest	Shareholder requirements in the long term	Company must maintain its existence	Concern re. security of investment: require capital growth
Multiple stakeholder obligations	Must manage requirements of many stakeholders	Prioritise stakeholders with high power and influence	Each stakeholder group expects interests to be understood and acted on
Shaper of society	How to deal with public interest obligations	Change society using positional power	Individuals only influence companies/ society as a group

Exam focus

Recent P1 questions on this topic include:

Topic	Pilot	D07	J08	D08	J09	D09	J10	D10	J11	D11	J12	D12	J13	D13	J14	D14
Absolutism/ relativism			Q2					Q1								
Deontological/ teleological	Q3			Q4									Q1			
Kohlberg CMD	SP Q1	Q1							Q1						Q4	
Social responsibility positions		Q4		Q1	Q2				Q1	Q4						Q1

*SP refers to supplementary pilot question paper

hapter

13

Professional and corporate ethics

In this chapter

- Profession and professionalism.
- Public interest.
- Accountants' role and influence.
- Corporate ethics.
- Professional codes of ethics.
- Conceptual framework and safeguards.
- Ethical dilemmas.
- Ethical conflict resolution.

Profession and professionalism

Profession

Definition

- A body of theory and knowlege which is used to support the public interest.

Professionalism

Definition

- Taking action to support the public interest.
- Acting professionally.

Views of professionalism

Reactive – noting negative aspects of accounting and taking action to remove those aspects e.g. legislation post Enron.

Proactive – seeking out new ways for accounting to support the public interest e self-imposed codes of conduct.

Public interest

Definition

That which supports the good of society as a whole (as opposed to what serves the interests of individual members of society or of specific sectional interest groups).

- Ethical codes confirm that acting against the public interest is not appropriate for an accountant.
- When considering whether to disclose information or not the accountant will need to evaluate each situation on its merits.

Accountants' role and influence

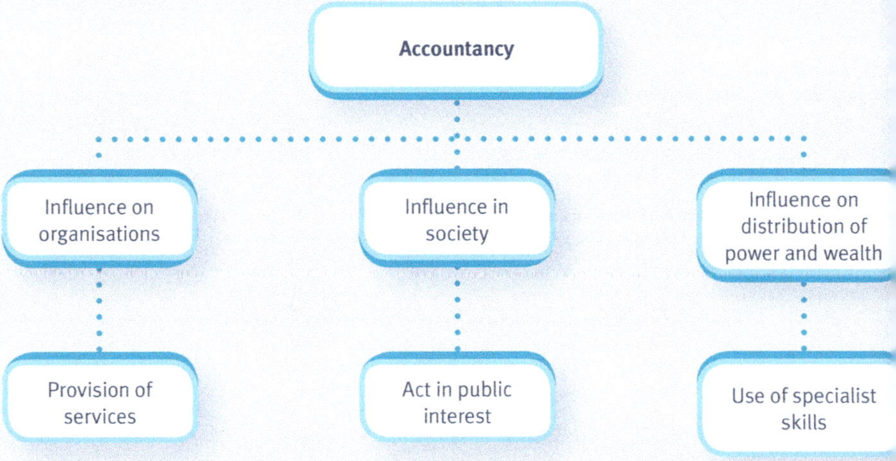

Limitations on influence:

Factor	Explanation
Extent of organisational reporting	'Negative' reporting on company in trading difficulties may cause company to close
Conflicts of interest in selling additional services	Cost-beneficial for the organisation and society – but undermines accountant's independence
Long-term relationships with clients	Long-term relationships means that the client is understood and better service provided – but may become too familiar limiting independence
Size of accountancy firms	Large firms reduce costs but may provide less personal service
Focus on growth and profit	Competition for services means costs fall – but care needed to ensure quality of service does not fall also

Definition

Corporate ethics

= application of ethical values to business behaviour.

How business ethics affects stakeholders

Shareholders

Expect fair and proper return on their investment. Company should provide this return and information on how shareholders investment managed

Suppliers

Suppliers attempt to provide quality goods on time. Company should pay invoices promptly, select suppliers on known criteria e.g. 'fair trade' principles

Wider community

Company affects society as a whole. CSR report explain how company treats wider community

Business values

Mission statement mentions

- products/services provided
- financial objectives
- role of business in society

Employees

How business relates to employees. Company recognises employee rights in areas such as working conditions, training, health and safety

Customer relations

Company has responsibility to produce quality goods/ services at reasonable price

Professional codes of ethics

Contents of code:

Introduction	Fundamental principles	Conceptual framework	Detailed application
States who code affects, how enforced	Key principles all members must follow	Explains how 'spirit' of principles applied	Principles applied to specific situations

Fundamental ethical principles

- **Integrity** – Members should be straightforward and honest in all professional/ business relationships
- **Objectivity** – Members do not allow bias or conflict of interest in business judgements
- **Competence** – Duty to maintain professional knowledge and skill at appropriate level
- **Confidentiality** – Information on clients not disclosed without appropriate specific authority
- **Professional behaviour** – Members must comply with relevant laws and avoid actions discrediting the profession

Conceptual framework and safeguards

Conceptual framework:

- provides initial set of values shared by those subject to the framework
- stated in general terms so easy to understand/communicate
- provides generalised guidelines – many issues have no 'correct' answer.

Ethical threats and safeguards

Threats = situation where person tempted not to follow code of ethics (see chapter 9 for exampl

Safeguards = guidance or course of action aimed at reducing or eliminating threats

Main safeguards include:

Profession	Work environment	Individual
• Education and training • CPD • Monitoring of work • Disciplinary proceedings	• Internal control systems • Review procedures • Codes of ethics • Disciplinary procedures	• Compliance with standards • Mentoring • Recording contentious issu • Assistance from profession body

Ethical dilemmas

Two main approaches.

Principles-based	Rules-based
Set of guidelines, individual interprets for specific situation	Set of rules – must be followed at all times
Benefits	
• Recognises cannot have rules for every situation • Allows for subjective judgement	• Easy to check compliance • Easy to amend rules
Disadvantages	
• Difficult to check compliance – individuals take different (but valid) actions	• Rule list does not cover every ethical situation • No room for individual decision making

Corruption and bribery

- Examples:
  - excessive 'hospitality'
  - facilitation payments
- it increases risk
- it is inherently unethical.

Relevant legislation

UK Bribery Act (2010)

- 4 offences
  - Offering, promising or giving bribe
  - Requesting, agreeing to receive c accepting a bribe.
  - Bribing a foreign public official.
  - A corporate offence of failing to prevent bribery.

Ethical conflict resolution

Factors to take into account in dealing with ethical conflict:

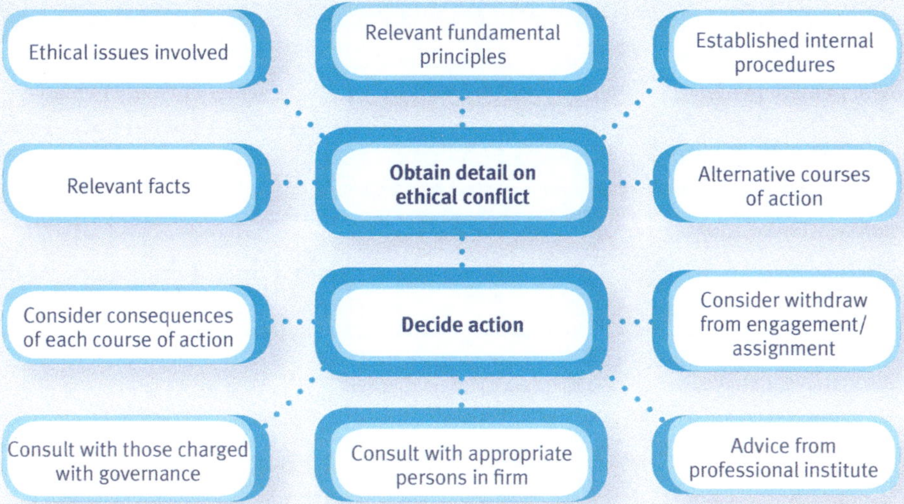

Exam focus

Recent P1 questions on this topic include:

Topic	Pilot	D07	J08	D08	J09	D09	J10	D10	J11	D11	J12	D12	J13	D13	J14
Professional	Q4		Q2			Q3	Q4				Q3	Q1			
Public interest					Q2		Q4		Q4						Q3
Professional codes	Q3				Q2	Q3	Q4							Q4	
Corporate codes				Q4					Q4						
Ethical conflict resolution						Q3									

hapter

14

Ethical decision making

In this chapter

- Ethical decision making frameworks.
- Stages of ethical decision making.
- Ethical behaviour.

Ethical decision making frameworks

Models provide a framework to assist in ethical decision making.

American Accounting Association

7 steps to making an ethical decision

1 What are the facts of the case?

2 What are the ethical issues in the case?

3 What are the norms, principles and values related to the case?

4 What are the alternative courses of action?

5 What is the best course of action that is consistent with the norms, principles and values identified in step 3?

6 What are the consequences of each possible course of action?

7 What is the decision?

Tucker's 5 questions

5 questions against which ethical decisio can be tested.

Is decision:

- Profitable?
- Legal?
- Fair?
- Right?
- Sustainable or environmentally sounc

Exam focus

Refer to examiner's article, published in Student Accountant, about ethics.

This will provide you with examples of the application of both of these models.

Stages of ethical decision making

4 stage process based on Kohlberg theory.

Model identifies

- Moral issue – knowing what is correct thing to do, and
- Moral behaviour – the actual action taken

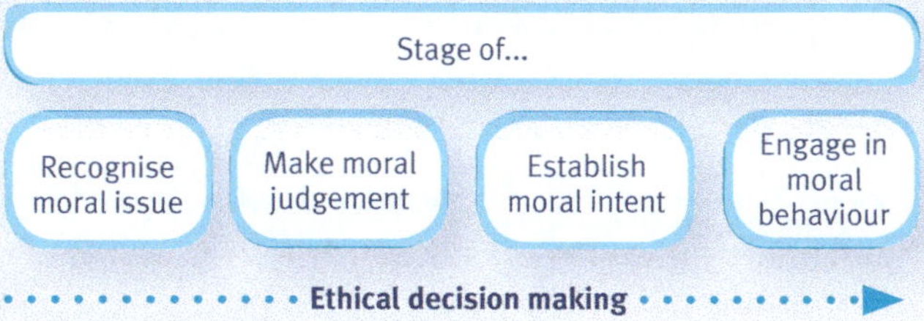

Ethical behaviour

Ability to make ethical decision depends on:

- issue related factors – how important decision is to decision-maker – factors affect moral intensity and moral framing.
- context-related factors – how factors relating to issue are viewed.

Factors affecting moral intensity

PROXIMITY
Nearness of decision maker to people affected by decision
'closer' increases moral intensity

CONCENTRATION OF EFFECT
How many people affected by action
Fewer people increases moral intensity

TEMPORAL IMMEDIACY
How soon effects of decision occur
Short time increases moral intensity

MAGNITUDE OF CONSEQUENCE
Extent of harm caused by poor advice
More harm increases moral intensity

SOCIAL CONSEQUENCES
Extent of agreement ethics of an action
More agreement increases moral intensity

PROBABILITY OF EFFECT
Likelihood harm/ benefit occurs
More likelihood increases moral intensity

Context-related factors:

- behaviour rewarded by superiors – even though dubious – will it be continued
- co-workers take same action – will it be continued.

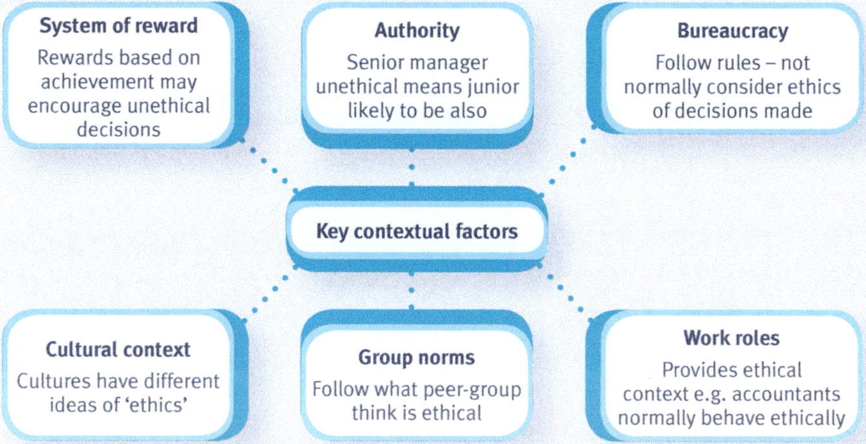

Exam focus

Recent P1 questions on this topic include:

Topic	Pilot	D07	J08	D08	J09	D09	J10	D10	J11	D11	J12	D12	J13	D13	J14	D
Tucker				Q1								Q4				
AAA						Q1					Q1					

hapter

15

Social and environmental issues

In this chapter

- Sustainability.
- Effects of economic activity.
- Accounting for sustainability.
- Internal management systems.
- Social and environmental audits.
- Social and environmental reporting.

Sustainability

Definition

Sustainability is an attempt to provide the best outcomes for the human and natural environments both now and into the indefinite future.

Definition

Sustainable development is development that meets the needs of the present without compromising the ability of future generations to meet their own needs.

Exam focus

This area is a popular topic in the compulsory scenario question. You may b required to discuss how the footprint of a organisation could be measured.

This definition of sustainability is also relevant to Tucker's decision making mod discussed in chapter 14.

Effects of economic activity

Definition

Environmental footprint = an attempt to evaluate the size of a company's impact on the environment in three respects:

- resource consumption
- pollution emissions
- measurement of both in terms of harm to the environment in qualitative, quantitative and replacement terms.

Definition

Social footprint = an evaluation of sustainability in terms of three areas of 'Anthro capital':

- social capital
- human capital
- constructed capital.

Accounting for sustainability

Methods of accounting for sustainability.

Full cost accounting	TBL accounting
Find total cost of company activities including environmental, economic and social costs.	Expand 'traditional' financial accounting to include environmental and social performan

Triple bottom line also explained in terms of:

People	Planet	Profit
Taking into account all stakeholder interests	Use of sustainable environmental practices	'Normal' profit measure use by non Triple Bottom Line (TBL) companies

Internal management systems

Businesses need to establish and maintain systems for assessing the organisation's impact on the environment.

Two main systems:

EMAS	**ISO 14000**
Eco-Management Audit Scheme – voluntary EU initiative to improve company performance.	Series of standards dealing with environmental management and supporting audit programme.
Rewards organisations who go beyond minimum legal requirements to improve environmental performance.	Specifies an Environmental Management System – company evaluated against this by audit and certified if meets standard.
Comply by initially implementing ISO 14000.	Comply by implementing an EMS and demonstrating compliance by audit.
Companies required to improve their environmental performance over time e.g. use less resources.	Companies must produce a plan for compliance with standard and monitor performance against planned objectives.

Social and environmental audits

Definition

Social audit = process enabling organisation to assess and demonstrate its social, economic a
environmental benefits and limitations.

Definition

Environmental audit = assessment of impact of the organisation on the environment.

- The audit provides the raw data for environmental accounting.
- It generally leads into an environmental action plan.

Three elements of an environment audit:

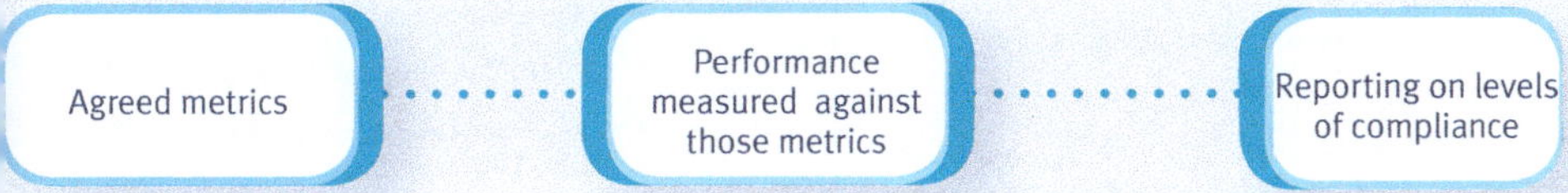

Exam focus

Refer to examiner's article, published in Student Accountant, on risk and environmental auditing.

Social and environmental reporting

Except in some highly regulated situations, the production of a social and environmental report is voluntary.

But what should companies report on?

Environmental reporting issues

- measures of emissions pollution, waste and greenhouse gases)
- consumption (e.g. of energy, water and non renewable mineral deposits).

Social reporting issues

- human rights
- work place, occupational health and safety
- training and employee issues
- fair pay for employees and suppliers
- fair business practices
- minority and equity issues
- marketplace and consumer issues.

Integrated reporting

Integrated Reporting demonstrates the linkages between an organisation's strategy, governance and financial performance and the social, environmental and economic context within which it operates.

Integrated Reporting can help business to take more sustainable decisions and enable investors and other stakeholders to understand how an organisation is really performing.

An Integrated Report should be a single report which is the organisation's primary report in most jurisdictions the Annual Report or equivalent.

Central to Integrated Reporting is the challenge facing organisations to create and sustain value inthe short, medium and longer term.

An integrated report is a concise communication about how an organisation's strategy, governance, performance and prospects, in the context of its external environment, lead to the creation of value in the short, medium and long term.

Five other types of sustainable capital

These are:

Manufactured capital
Material goods, or fixed assets which contribute to the production process rather than being the output itself – e.g. tools, machines and buildings.

Intellectual capital
This form of capital can be described as the value of a company or organisation's employee knowledge, business training and any proprietary information that may provide the company with a competitive advantage.

(NB: Some of the subsets of intellectual capital include human capital, information capital, brand awareness and instructional capital.)

Human capital
This can be described as consisting of people's health, knowledge, skills and motivation. Enhancing human capital thro education and training is central.

Social capital
This can be described as being concerne with the institutions that help us maintain and develop human capital in partnership with others; e.g. families, communities, businesses.

Natural capital
This can be described as any stock or flo energy and material within the environme that produces goods and services e.g. climate regulation, climate change, CO2 emissions.

Value creation process

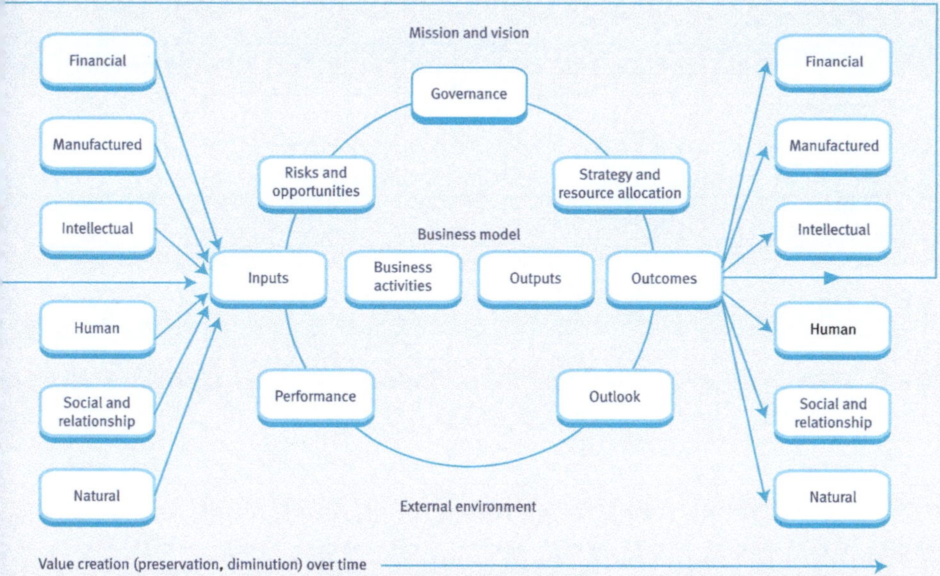

Exam focus

Recent P1 questions on this topic include:

Topic	Pilot	D07	J08	D08	J09	D09	J10	D10	J11	D11	J12	D12	J13	D13	J14
Environmental footprint	Q1						Q1			Q1		Q1			
Sustainability			Q1					Q2		Q1				Q1	Q3
Integrated reporting															

Index

A

B

C

D

E

F

G

H

I

J

K

M

N

U

V

Notes

Notes

Notes

Notes

Notes

Notes

Notes

Notes

Notes

Notes

Notes

Notes

Notes

Notes